D0197337

Living Simple, Free & Happy

How to Simplify, Declutter Your Home, and Reduce Stress, Debt, and Waste

Cristin Frank

BETTERWAY HOME
CINCINNATI, OHIO
WWW.BETTERWAYBOOKS.COM

Contents

Introduction

How well are you using your talents? Pause. Now ask yourself how well you're using your time. Stretch it a little further and ask how well you are using the space in your home. You may think these aspects of life (talents, time, and space) are a bit unrelated, but the truth is these three elements closely work together to combat stress, improve efficiencies, relieve money woes, open up opportunities, and provide unbelievable self-fulfillment. The keys that unlock all this potential are empowering your abundant talents (trust me, you have a ton of talent), maximizing your free time, and giving yourself space to create, entertain, and just put up your feet.

As a culture, we have escalated into a lifestyle of bigger homes, more stuff, and countless activities and appointments. This sounds like a full life—a life so full it's overflowing with obligations, chaos, and maintenance instead of happiness. It's a life filled with the wrong stuff. This book will guide you in creating a life full of meaning by reducing all of the stuff that's impeding your way to greatness. I'm going to walk you through the joys of discovering your pride, help you appreciate what you have and what it can become, and talk you through the fears that limit the potential of your home, finances, and your sense of purpose.

When you think about simplifying your life, you may hesitate because you're focusing on what you're giving up. This book will show you all you have to gain from streamlining your calendar, becoming self-sufficient, and opting for creativity instead of spending. And you're not going it alone. No way. The reduction plan invites opportunities for you to bring your friends and family into your world of exploration and discovery. You will find like-minded people who share your passion for self-empowerment. I know this because I've been there, trying to do my own thing, and I have found others out there with great stories and creations to share.

Learning is Leadership

If there is one principle of the reduction lifestyle I would impress upon you, it is continuous learning. Learning is rarely a passive thing. It's that inner drive that helps you keep an open mind and makes you try something new or initiate an introduction to a stranger. The crazy part is we never reach an end in our learning. There is always something new to learn and do. I find that fascinating. Seriously, I get jacked about it. Are you with me? Don't you want to know all that's out there?

The fact that you're reading this book is a huge testament to your commitment to seek knowledge. I am so emphatic about learning because it facilitates leadership in our lives. I'm not talking about the Moses kind of lead-

> This is a lifestyle course in which you will learn to create with the purpose of clearing out the clutter and eliminating the debt and maintenance that are weighing you down.

ership; I'm talking about leading your *own* life. My goal in this book is not to teach you how to live your life just like I live mine. My hope is to open your eyes to new possibilities that will put you in a position to solve your own problems, make your own decisions, and achieve your higher goals. How you apply this new information to your life is entirely up to you.

Aren't you curious about all the amazing things you are capable of doing? This book includes numerous how-to projects ranging from basic household tasks to full upcycling makeovers. Rest assured, if I can do it, you can certainly do it, too. And not only does the book guide you through the reduction metamorphosis, it features exercises throughout so you can personalize the lessons on paper and implement them as they relate to your life and specific needs. Keep in mind, this is not a book full of "neat" projects. This is a lifestyle course in which you will learn to create with the purpose of clearing out the clutter and eliminating the debt and maintenance that are weighing you down. These projects are three-fold: use your talents to create something useful and inexpensive or free that improves your home.

This book will help you take charge for yourself. Buck the cycle of mindless entertainment, disposable everything, and the infatuation with what others have. Your time and money don't need to be invested in ways that please or compete with other people; invest these resources in yourself for an outcome that guarantees satisfaction for you.

Decisions Lead to Freedom

The small, daily decisions you make result in either your freedom from or entrapment by clutter, stress, and debt. The problem is, we rarely recognize when we are making these decisions. Emotions are so powerful that they dictate our actions in an automated fashion. That is why we need to work backwards. This book will help you achieve the results you desire and allow you to make the decisions that get you where you want to go. When you decide where you want to be, you can customize a plan to get yourself there. What is it that you love, respect, and appreciate? These are your values. They're the filters that will replace toxic emotions when it comes to making decisions. And while our goals and values vary widely from life stage to life stage, when you look at the big picture, the common threads of purpose, pride, freedom, and quality run through every stage. This book brings to life the expectations we have when it comes to enjoying our surroundings and relieving the pressures that rush at us through life. Decide to slow down. Decide to let go of what is weighing on you and your environment.

When we say we want it all, we don't necessarily mean a boat, a lake house, and a butler. That isn't the standard of success. Success is getting what we want, that one great thing we can call our own. It's putting our energy into our dreams and interests. So get ready to trade in headaches and hassles for life skills; exchange clutter for money; transform eyesores into beautiful focal points in your home; say goodbye to over-consumption and hello to genuine experiences.

Welcome.

1: Ropes on a Blimp

Have you ever thought that maybe what is holding you back is what you have and not what you don't have? When we think of roadblocks, the excuses that surface sound something like, "I just don't have the time; I'm swamped…I'd need more education…or plastic surgery." How often do we find ourselves saying, "You need money to do that"? It's so easy to look at what we don't have instead of examining our spending and consumption habits to see if they are keeping us in a vicious cycle of spending, accumulating, and maintaining.

Peers, advertisers, and society suggest you live it up at all stages of life. Graduates, don't you owe it to yourself to indulge after eating cafeteria food and driving a rust bucket for four years? Or in your thirties and forties, when your income is at its peak, isn't this the time to pamper yourself? How about in your fifties and sixties when your kids have moved out? You can finally have nice things that won't get wrecked by vomit and hockey pucks. If not then...when? The more prudent (though far less sexy) approach is to exercise more financial discipline (more saving, smarter investing, and wiser spending habits) during times of increased pay and less dependencies. Just because you lived through times of sacrifice doesn't mean you over-compensate when your situation changes. If you forgo your morning coffee, you don't drink ten Red Bulls with lunch. And because you're making 20 percent more doesn't mean you should increase your luxuries by the full 20 percent to make up for lost time. You don't need to repay your ego. If you max out with your upswings, you're going to bottom out with your downturns. Trying to continually adapt to a yo-yo lifestyle will be much more traumatizing than staying even keel on a track to what you really want.

Just because you lived through times of sacrifice doesn't mean you over-compensate when your situation changes.

So many people think buckets of money will solve or eliminate the stresses in life. Such is not the case. More is more and less is less. In other words, the more you bring into your life, the more you have to maintain. If you are accumulating things, the initial purchase is just the beginning. In addition to any debt you took on to make the purchase, this new item you now own may need to be stored, dusted, watered, cleaned, oiled, tightened, filled, emptied, refilled, tuned, insured, renewed—or any number of other time-consuming (and possibly expensive) maintenance chores. If you avoid the purchase altogether, you cut out the chain reaction of obligations to this thing. So does this mean you pack it all up, live a super-minimalist lifestyle and never purchase anything again? No, absolutely not. It simply means you recognize all your options and make fully educated decisions about how and what you consume. This book will open your eyes to possibilities you might never have considered.

Common, everyday decisions and behaviors often result in wasted time, space, and money. This book will show you consumption alternatives that will streamline your lifestyle and increase your talents. If you follow these principles, you'll rid your home and your schedule from clutter that is holding you back. You'll have more free time and your life will be maximized for efficiency, self-fulfillment, and opportunities for enrichment. This is what I term a reduction lifestyle—reduce excessive consumption, unnecessary obligations, and overbearing clutter. When you reduce the waste, you are free to dedicate yourself to exactly what you want and how you want to live. You will love what you have and who you are.

Principles of Reduction

Reduction can be a scary word. What does it mean to embrace a lifestyle of reduction? Does it require constant sacrifice and self-denial? No way! When you finish this book, I promise you will still be able to live with yourself and continue to enjoy all the conveniences, hobbies, and interests you do now.

The secret is to focus on what you are gaining rather than what you are giving up.

The secret is to focus on what you are gaining rather than what you are giving up. Yes, you may be giving up the opportunity to own a shiny new gadget, but you are gaining (or retaining) open space in your home (that new gadget will need to live somewhere), open time in your schedule (you would need to maintain or play with the gadget), and money in your bank account (you keep all the money you don't spend).

Some of the reduction lifestyle principles we'll explore are:

- How to make your home and lifestyle a reflection of your talents
- How to increase your personal freedom by detaching yourself from things
- What being original means to your bottom line and self-esteem
- Where to look for cash, savings, and peace of mind
- How to say "no" without a guilt trip
- How to find the potential for function and beauty in the things you already own
- How to eliminate debt and still have the things you want

- How to love the process of streamlining your schedule and possessions (my personal favorite)

The lifestyle of reduction is a commitment to your values. And the fun
you have, the skills you acquire, the space you create, and the stress you
relieve along the way will surprise you. Cutting out the crap is truly a risk-
free program.

A Pile of Clutter or a Pile of Cash?

What if I told you the average homeowner has five thousand dollars worth
of unused or unwanted stuff in his or her home? Would you be interested in
finding it? You bet you would! Now I'm not suggesting you should sell your
kitchen table. I'm suggesting you sell the stuff piled on your kitchen table
or in your coat closet, basement, and drawers (I call these places the grave-
yards of once-useful-and-desired belongings), aka the clutter that is always
in your way, making your house feel messy and disorganized.

Internet sites such as Craigslist, eBay, Amazon and MyClozet.net are
driving much higher prices for items that were once sold for next to nothing
at garage sales. And networking sites aren't just for socializing; people use
them to seek deals, post and find jobs, swap information, promote goods,
and announce services. A boy in the boonies no longer has to leave his car
to rust with a For Sale sign in the window. He can make himself a global
retailer with the help of a computer and a digital camera. There are no pre-
requisites for entry into the global economy. All are invited and encouraged.
Instead of writing broken items off as worthless junk, find your pride, fix
them up, and sell them for extra cash.

If your stuff is broken, damaged, or missing a part, fix it. Paint it using
a new technique from a magazine or with some leftover paint you already
have sitting in your garage. Go online and order the missing part. Sometimes, a small piece of plastic can transform a useless item into something
you can sell for a hundred dollars. How do I know? A friend of ours gave us
a telescope that his kids had left in the rain. It was high-resolution with a
digital star finder. The only problems were the missing lens caps and rusty
battery cage. We acquired the telescope for free, and for a year, it sat in my
house, unused and broken. I finally decided to do something with it and
discovered that if the telescope were in working order, it would be quite

valuable. So I did some investigating. I spent seventeen dollars on parts and used some tin foil to clean out the rust on the battery connector. After these minor repairs, we were able to sell the telescope for 150 dollars. Chapter four will introduce you to some basic repair skills, while chapter five will give you more ideas on how you can find items to repurpose and repair.

Contrary to what you may be thinking, nothing is holding you back from reclaiming your closet space or getting out of debt. You don't need to be a skilled craftsman, just willing to learn. I was allergic to power tools until I went to a free workshop at Home Depot. Now I'm very comfortable with a drill. After I bought a ten-dollar sewing machine at an estate sale, I asked my mom to show me how to use it. I stuck notes next to every knob and lever on the machine until I felt comfortable with what I was doing. I've calculated that I save about five hundred dollars each year by using my sewing machine to make gifts, curtains, clothes, and costumes, and to repair shoes and garments. It doesn't matter what level you start at; your craftsmanship will improve with practice; just don't get frustrated.

Reclaiming Your Time

You may be thinking, *That's great for you, but I just don't have time to repair things or do it myself.* I'm a sensible person. I can understand that you may be short on time. Because it's limited, time is our most precious commodity, but it's also equally available. Do you really need a hairstyle that takes you forty minutes each morning to perfect? Do you need to live in the next county over from your office? Time is money, but it's also about decisions. And when you sit back and truly evaluate your situation, you'll find that you do have control over these decisions. Believe me, taking the time to save money is a lot more fun than the many options available for making money! However, when you take time to save money, you may find yourself with new options to make money. For example, learning to sew your own curtains means you can also sew curtains that someone can buy from you. Mastering the ability to save money while looking for opportunities to make money makes you an unstoppable force.

A good chunk of this book is about time because it relates directly to our freedom. Time, finite and uncertain, is really our most precious gift. Our goal here is to modify time in our daily lives—doing less of what we don't like and more of what we do like. Time is a constant, regardless of what we do. That's why I'm going to show you how you can also be thrifty with your time. A reduction in lifestyle that upholds your values will give you back the time you need and want to spend with loved ones, perfect your talents, and have more fun. Your schedule is exactly that: *your* schedule. How often do you say, "Let me check my schedule," but what you're really checking is to see if you can serve someone else's schedule. Everyone tries to get you on their schedules, and if you let them, your time will be pulled in their direction. It may be more comfortable to simply go along on someone else's schedule, but it won't be easier, and it often won't be in your best interest. By the end of this book, you'll learn how to live by these two Reduction Rebel truths:

> A reduction in lifestyle that upholds your values will give you back the time you need and want to spend with loved ones, perfect your talents, and have more fun.

1. We all choose how we spend our time.
2. We have a right to say no to activities (even fun activities) that don't fit our schedules.

Throughout this book, I'll debunk all of your time and scheduling issues so you can focus on your agenda. As you start cutting back, especially in your schedule, you may find yourself making excuses for your decisions, but don't cower to the pressures or expectations of others. You don't have to evangelize or apologize; you just need to set boundaries and expectations. By abiding by this guide on your crusade as a Reduction Rebel, you will experience personal satisfaction and financial achievement, and you'll be a heck of a lot more interesting.

Do you ever get asked, "What have you done lately"? What's your typical response? It's probably something like "not much." Now you know that's not true. The reality is you've been so busy you haven't had a minute to yourself. You're probably constantly on the go, but everything you've been doing has been for someone or something else. Your days are full of menial tasks that don't interest you, and because they don't interest you, you know they won't interest anyone else. Why do we let ourselves live this way?

Have you ever heard someone say, "Oh, you've gotta check out this awesome birdhouse I made"? That person has carved out time for her interest. She's enjoying her time, and because she finds it enjoyable and interesting, she knows other people will be interested, too. You're going to be that person. When someone asks you what you've been up to, you'll be able to share how you've indulged in your interests. Your days will have meaning, and you'll feel real accomplishment at the end of each one. You will know the stimulation that comes from creativity. You're going to notice your house coming together and your skills developing, and you'll have stories to tell about the things you have and the places you've been. You will buzz about your quilt making, furniture refinishing, recycled jewelry enterprise, or closet organization. It feels good. Believe me. Using your skills and having tangible accomplishments at the end of the day will expose sincere satisfaction and an unbelievable sense of pride.

Using your skills and having tangible accomplishments at the end of the day will expose sincere satisfaction and an unbelievable sense of pride.

My Origins as a Reduction Rebel

So how did I come to write this book? What have I done differently? Well, in our late twenties, my husband and I had something catastrophic come into our lives. It was no accident, and for a moment, we accepted it. And, heck, we were pretty excited about it—more excited about it than anything that had come before it. We even have Christmas ornaments celebrating it. One might call it the American dream—an investment and stability all in one. The catastrophe was the purchase of our home.

We had added our house to the list of other large debts, like our student loans and a leased SUV. Our debt commitment was planned on a manageable schedule. We just needed to make payments plus interest until we retired. Oh joy. We were in our twenties, for goodness sake, and we had just tied ourselves to debt that was going to take us the better part of our adult lives to pay off. We went from educated, carefree twenty-somethings with limitless possibilities to knowing exactly how we were going to spend the next thirty years—working continually to pay off debts. Instantly, that time was planned for us. Talk about your life passing before you! We knew everyone on every street like ours was in the same situation, but we couldn't accept it. By the time we actually owned our house, we were going to be gray and our kids would be gone. Sure, a routine can provide a sense of stability, but it's terribly boring. We pigeonholed ourselves as worker bees in a gigantic hive that's fueling the economy. We were now part of the middle class.

Did I mention that we had practically no furniture? We returned wedding presents to get cash to buy a couch. And we knew if we were going to furnish the rest of our 1900-square-foot house, we were going to go even further into debt. This was a serious situation. We had jumped right onto life's treadmill—a slippery slope of socially dictated needs that compiled debt, consumption and, the silent killer, maintenance. Why hadn't we seen this coming?

Unfortunately, the common American is a mass consumer. Somewhere it became natural to mega-consume, which means accumulating debt and clutter, and filling weekends with running errands. Buy now, pay later. It's our culture; it's how we were raised. But after we had debt hanging over our heads, my husband and I changed our tune on buying more and more. Consumption was not our friend. Quickly, we became acutely aware of our financial commitments, and sitting back and accepting indefinite payments, like everyone else had, made us ill. Our debt was at the forefront of our consciousness. We made spreadsheets on what we had, stacked against what we owed. Paycheck to paycheck, the balance of debt barely budged. We knew what we were up against. We just needed a game plan.

Exploring Our Options

We put our heads together to come up with an approach for tackling our financial burden. We had a lot of options. One quick fix was to just sell our house and reverse the predicament we'd gotten ourselves in. But what were we going to do then? Live in a mobile home in our friend's backyard? That wouldn't solve anything.

We entertained the idea of being minimalists because we had one car and no cell phone, but when it came to living space, we had to be practical. We could get comfortable with this home and grow into it, or we could move into a smaller one and upgrade with every change in life. Three months into our marriage, I was pregnant with our first son, so the time was right for the house we were in; we just had to get smart about our money and our decisions—all of our decisions. Money was only one factor. If we were going to work every angle to pay off our debt, we also needed to look at what else was cramming our schedule. We couldn't devote 24/7 to financial freedom; there had to be some personal fulfillment in there, too.

One obvious solution to combating our debt woes was to find higher paying jobs. Climbing the corporate ladder invariably meant more stress, longer hours, and more travel for the salary increase. That was something that we just couldn't get excited about, though as college grads, career advancement was in our psyche. It could take years to get a break or find a higher position, but we had plenty of time…thirty years to be exact. In the end, the idea of a bigger salary seemed to go hand in hand with accumulating a bigger everything. But that was someone else's plan, not ours.

Early in our battle with debt, we were attracted to self-employment options. We could start our own business, play the stock market, or invest in real estate. The champions of risk had strong arguments: buy assets, accumulate good debt, reinvest your dividends, and eventually go public. They were slick and savvy. They were master salesmen and aggressive business types. They pushed to get more stuff to fund the other stuff in your life. We got hyped about the prospect of four-hour workweeks and rental home acquisitions, but our action plans were feeble and hesitant. So many self-help resources boast about how easy it is to attract cash flow. We had all the CDs on being rich, but for us, it wasn't something we could jump into immediately. Facing the responsibilities posed by married life, our new house, and a baby on the way was about all we could handle. It wasn't like we were going to start a franchise the next day. Biting off more than we could manage would not have been a pleasant solution. We couldn't act like we had nothing to lose when we had spent our whole lives in school and were on the brink of parenthood. Plus, more is more. We didn't really want to start escalating our lifestyle of more work, more stuff, more obligations. The honest truth boiled down to: we needed to stay close to our comfort zone.

The flip side of an all-out investment onslaught was to squirrel away a small percentage of income and invest it in safe mutual funds. We would ignore that money for decades and then after all that time, discover that we had lots of money to slowly withdraw in our old age. Although this method has you adapt to a little bit less than what you actually make, it takes forever. This option has been referred to as "automatic" because your savings are automated, not because you're automatically rich. Although this is a sound plan, it couldn't be our only plan. It's a very comfortable, low-maintenance solution, but it's not going to do you any favors in terms of time.

The most proactive, take-charge-without-losing-your-shirt solution for us was to live below our means but within our values. It was easier for us to take a hard look at what we were doing, what we already had, and simply reduce.

What does that look like? Well, it's an evaluation of needs versus wants, taking into consideration respect for yourself and others. To live below your means involves funding your future, not your past. In other words, pay for what you can afford when you can afford it.

Do you remember when there were no credit cards? Me either. So we have to have some inner gauge of what we have and what we want, what we need and what unexpected circumstance is waiting to surprise us. (Whoops, the dishwasher just quit working. Didn't see that coming.) Some people call this a budget; I'm not really into budgeting. I'm more of a strict evaluator. Needs really need to be needs. I know when to make an exception, and I have the sense to know what is ridiculous.

> To live below your means involves funding your future, not your past.

Can you prolong gratification? Of course you can; you just might be out of practice. Can you believe that there is more around the corner? Sure, I'm going to prove it to you! This book is about showing you a path that doesn't involve risk, radical sacrifice, or blissful ignorance. There are two ways to measure success: what you do and what you don't do. Our success is what we did with our creativity and what we didn't do with our money and time. We used our talents to be self-sufficient. We used creativity to upcycle things we already had or could get for next to nothing. We didn't accept a thirty-year mortgage or see the need for two cars and a home full of showroom furniture and overflowing closets, cabinets, and storage areas.

Freedom from clutter, debt, waste, and stress will be yours if you hold to the lifestyle of reduction and values. To show you how powerful this shift was for us, consider this fact: We fully furnished our home and paid off our mortgage in six years and eight months. So by our midthirties, we had eliminated our school loans, car payments, and mortgage. We were 100 percent debt-free. I didn't mention credit cards because we never carried a balance on them. We used them and paid them off each month. And I never cut them up either. They're convenient, especially for e-commerce. (Yes, you can use debit cards online, but we take advantage of the extra security and cash-back rewards.) I think that walking around with wads of cash in my pocket is pretty silly. I can safely say I'm responsible enough to have a credit card.

> I went to art school, so please make no misjudgment of me being a financial guru. Also, make no misjudgments of your own financial potential, no matter your background.

Please don't think we stopped living in the process. We took family vacations every year, Clark W. Griswold style, and had plenty of fun along the way. Our memories are not of strife and sacrifice. We had a blast and became closer as a family.

I applied my innate creativity to save money, create useful items for my home, and even to make money off of things that were taking up space and, more important, my precious time. I'm not going to give investment advice, except when it comes to investing in your abilities. Relying on yourself to fix a dresser drawer, cook a healthy meal, or make up a room for a special guest are qualities of character that never lose value.

Don't Forget to Water

This book will take you through a series of decisions. Your task is to apply them consistently. You'll be looking at things and situations objectively and be your own authority on what is right for you. You'll be able to get your momentum going and stay focused on your goal of cutting out the junk, paying off the debt that's keeping you from true freedom and gaining life skills that keep you jazzed about living.

It works as much as you want it to—kind of like flossing. My dentist imparted this sage wisdom on me once: "Just floss the teeth you want to keep." Cheeky guy, huh? The same is true for applying common sense and moderation to your lifestyle. The areas that you put energy into are the areas where you will see results. I will share practical advice and information that you can use immediately with lasting effects on your life. I ask only that you put a little thought into how you want to personally apply the principles so they custom fit your life. Tailoring to your specific needs will help you streamline in a way that's manageable for you so you can start living as a Reduction Rebel, aka a Freedomist. (Yes, I made up the word Freedomist, but the reduction lifestyle is by far the least expensive ticket to freedom.)

We'll look at how you "spend" the space in your home, the time in your day, and the money in your bank account. You will learn to challenge the growing myths and alienation of the human spirit that have become ever present in today's society. Through careful self-examination, you become aware of the many layers of life that serve only as a burden (I call this baggage). What we've accumulated is restricting our freedoms. I'm not advocating you move into a lean-to and eat only canned goods. I'll show you how to position yourself so you can create things and savor what is truly important. Ultimately, a reduction in lifestyle allows you to live as you choose. That's true freedom.

Relying on yourself to fix a dresser drawer, cook a healthy meal, or make up a room for a special guest are qualities of character that never lose value.

2: Life as a Reduction Rebel

"Less is more" is a common saying. Another slogan is, "Whoever dies with the most toys wins." Sadly, more people live as if the latter saying were true, and they spend their lives accumulating more and more things. The Reduction Rebel knows better and follows the first principle. This chapter will show you how to reduce the clutter in your schedule and in your home. You'll also learn how to reduce your consumer habits so you can save money and space in your home while reducing the amount of waste you contribute to landfills.

So what is a Reduction Rebel? Reduction Rebels are people who increase their free time and the amount of open space in their homes by reducing how much they consume socially and financially. They make these reductions by setting boundaries and goals for how they use their time and by reusing, recycling, and repurposing items in their home. This lifestyle combines principles of financial and ecological conservation (save money, spare Mother Earth) with creative expression. Reduction Rebels make investments in their talents and abilities to understand what is possible. Do they resist the norm? Only when the norm goes against their values.

Identify Your Values

So what do Reduction Rebels value? Most important, they value quality time with the people they love and time to discover and develop their interests and talents in ways that bring them satisfaction.

They strive to do things for themselves in the spirit of independence, but not necessarily independent from people. Reduction Rebels strive to be independent and uncontrolled by bad habits that cost them money, time, health, and self-satisfaction. They know when to say yes and how to say no.

Ask yourself, *what is the purpose of my life?* Look inside yourself for the answer. When you find the answer, you'll find it much easier to distinguish between what is and is not important to you. You'll know what you value, so you can eliminate from your life everything you don't value and more fully focus on what is important to you. I'm not going to tell you what you should and shouldn't value, and I'm not going to tell you what you should and shouldn't keep in your life. It's your life. Make the decisions for yourself.

We all have expectations for ourselves. Self-expectations put you in the driver's seat to success. What are you capable of? The answer is, a whole lot, believe me.

Reduce the Clutter in Your Home

In the 1980s, my grandparents used to take me to the Adirondack Mountains for a week in the summertime. This was where I was first introduced to life without television, water conservation (if it's yellow, let it mellow; if it's brown, flush it down), and the garbage dump. Up in the mountains, the landfill was a spectator sport. It was the Roman Coliseum of Upstate New

Exercise

Metaphorical gnats swarm around our head every day. These are the distractions that slow us down and take us away from what we really want to do. What is getting in your way? Is there something physically in the way blocking your path or view? Is there an attitude or belief holding you back? Do an honest assessment and make a list of these things. Now evaluate that list and identify where you can make a positive change to eliminate the problem. For example, are there solutions you can employ that will improve the flow of your morning routine or evening runaround?

York. We would take our weekly garbage to the landfill and watch—from a safe distance—bears come out and eat it. What a concept for an impressionable mind: black bears eat all our garbage. Isn't the symbiosis terrific! If only that were true. In everyday life we are not just throwing away beef gristle and melon rinds. We're throwing away everything from bubble wands to sleeper sofas. That stuff isn't part of the food chain. It has to go somewhere.

First it comes from somewhere, then we have our time with it, then it goes somewhere. And this cycle is snowballing through our ecosystem. Our lifestyle has ballooned into commodities times one hundred and luxuries times ten. We've proved that it is possible to consume on these mass scales. But we know we cannot maintain it, and we especially cannot store it. Like time, our space is limited, too.

Resources -> Product -> Waste

Therefore, we have one serendipitous solution: reduce.

Visiting a landfill as a kid was one very literal experience of viewing our waste in the world, but it took me a lot longer to notice waste that wasn't leaving my house. When I said waste goes somewhere, I wasn't necessarily talking about dumping it in the ocean. What about the waste that we hold on to? The waste that we trip over. The waste that hides the car keys from us. These aren't problems that you can leave for the tree huggers of the world. This is our personal waste that is inhibiting our movement and energy.

The Catastrophes of Clutter

We are sabotaging our personal environment through mass consumption. Let's set aside aesthetics. There are some downright dangers involved with having too much stuff in our homes. And I'm not talking about homes that qualify for the TV show *Hoarders*. I'm talking about ramifications to everyday life from having too much stuff lying around.

Clutter all over your house can make you trip and fall. Are you going to die, or even go to the hospital? Probably not. But think of the bruises you've gotten from clutter avalanches in overcrowded closets. Now think about getting out of your house in a fire. Most likely it's dark, and you're definitely panicked. This is not the time to regret the laundry piles on the stairs or the coats thrown on the floor below the already encumbered coat rack. More than twenty-five million Americans will experience a house fire this year. It does happen.

It's no secret that car emissions are causing poor air quality. The same could be said for clutter in our home. Take, for example, the numerous bottles of personal care products sitting on the ledge of the tub. Those bottles trap moisture—moisture that sits there for months sometimes. That is a breeding ground for mold and mildew, which can contaminate the air quality in your home. Now that's just one location of moisture. How about all the sinks around your house? Take a look at what is hanging around your water sources. You might want to bring your rubber gloves.

Mold and mildew are not the only toxins harbored in your clutter. Think of all the added surface area clutter gives to dust. Even if you dust every week there is no way to reach all the dust in every corner, bookcase, and tabletop. Seriously, who wants more things to dust in the first place?

Lastly, I've got to say it: bugs. Clutter nurtures breeding grounds. Let's see, popular squatters include maggots, ants, biting mites, mice, and cockroaches. No thank you.

Studies have been done that relate clutter to cognitive issues in children. Too much visual and physical disorder can affect a child's ability to focus. If you've ever looked into remedies for a fussy baby, you may know that experts recommend clearing out their environment—even using black-and-white décor to limit visual noise in the environment.

Adults have similar mental responses to clutter. It can cause neurosis.

Symptoms include worrying, the inability to make a decision, and an overall interpersonal imbalance, all of which slow you down and can even fuel consumption. This becomes an emotional cycle that deepens the problems and effects.

By reducing clutter in our homes, we eliminate drains on our time, health and emotions. And by doing so, we open ourselves up to the many benefits of open spaces.

Displacing the Waste

The universe and everything in it is prone to entropy. Therefore, may I suggest Mark Twain's quote be tweaked to, the only *three* certainties in life are *death*, *taxes*, and *disorder*. And it seems that there is no greater uphill battle than fighting the degeneration of our dwellings. Whether you're a homeowner or renter, the laundry and mail still accumulate, light bulbs burn out, and belongings become outdated. It's a fact of life: we're human beings who like change. We will always have things in our home that lose luster, relevance, and appeal. We are not going to use a baby stroller forever. Clothes shrink, or we grow. Technology evolves. And everything that is outdated becomes clutter.

Get rid of your excess. Keep only what you use and love. This doesn't have to be a painful experience; it can be an exciting money-making opportunity.

If you have clutter, start purging. Get rid of your excess. Keep only what you use and love. This doesn't have to be a painful experience; it can be an exciting money-making opportunity. Remember when I said the average home is sitting on about five thousand dollars worth of unwanted stuff? Now is your time to cash in. As you purge, keep in mind that Reduction Rebels limit what they keep in their lives, but they also limit what they contribute to landfills. Don't just throw things away to get rid of them. Sell your unwanted items online or through consignment. Or give them to friends or donate them to charity. Chapter three is full of ideas for how to sell or swap your unwanted clutter, and it will also help you deal with the emotional attachments you have to your belongings.

Or fully embrace the Reduction Rebel lifestyle and brainstorm ways to transform what you have into what you need. Chapter five is full of ideas for repurposing old household items. I love to look at something and imagine what it can become or who would enjoy it more. It feels good to revive what's old or broken down; to give away something that someone else will appreciate; to make money off the junk that's taking up valuable space. This is where the real fun happens.

Intake Reduction

After you purge, keep clutter from returning by curbing your consumption. Limit yourself to only what you need. Yes, those holiday dishes are cute, but is it worth the space and financial investment to use them twice a year and store them the other eleven months?

The secret to keeping your home organized is to have a place for everything and put everything in its place. Why is this easier said than done? Because if we are honest, we often don't have enough room to create proper homes for everything we own, so we just leave it lying out because there's no better place for it. Clutter is evidence of excess.

If you have a limited number of Tupperware pieces, it will be easy to put them away and easy to find matching lids and containers when you need them. The same is true with anything else in your home—clothes, remote controls, movies, and especially toys. The less you have, the easier it is to care for and use. You also get more return on your investment because you get more use out of the item.

> Clutter is evidence of excess.

You have control over what you bring into your house, but what about what others bring to you? If you have children, you know how birthdays and holidays can create a landslide of presents that your house can't accommodate. See the Five Alternatives to Gift Giving sidebar for creative gift ideas you can request family and friends give your children.

A Place for Everything

Having a place for everything and a sequence for tasks requires setting up systems: the mail goes from the mailbox to be sorted on the counter; junk is recycled, bill due dates are marked on the calendar, and the paperwork is put in a container on the computer desk. Don't even take the mail out of the mailbox if you don't have the two minutes it takes to follow through on

Five Alternatives to Gift Giving

1. *Donate to a Cause:* This doesn't have to be as passive as you may think. For instance, zoos and animal shelters are always looking for food and supplies. Do a little research (female sloths love mushrooms). Ask your guests to bring items from your "Zookeeper's Shopping List." This can tie into many fun party themes and actively help out a great cause.

2. *Fifteen Minutes of Fame:* Let your guest of honor and his or her guests share a story, poem, recipe, or picture. If it's a kid's party, make enough copies for everyone and then have an autograph session. Being almost famous can be as fun as getting gifts.

3. *Make an Investment:* Ask your guests to contribute to a 529 or savings account. Or let your kid be a junior stock investor. Check out www.oneshare.com where you can buy someone his or her very first share of stock. You can even send it framed with a personalized, engraved nameplate. A more tangible idea is a proof set of coins from a birth year.

4. *Create on Canvas:* Take a blank or partially designed canvas and let the group add their creative expressions and imagery. Friendship art will weather the storms of time, trends, and maturity.

5. *I Have Just the Ticket:* Instead of a physical gift, give an experience, such as admission to a movie, theatre, museum, or an expo.

these steps. This type of procedure goes for everything from homework to permission slips to laundry to car keys.

Think about the things that often follow the words, "Where's the…" What things are you always searching for? The TV remote, scissors, keys, purse? These things need consistency; otherwise you will always be searching for them. Establish a home for these things, and always return them to their home when not in use. Make this a family activity. Everyone in your household needs to be on board and in the know. Use labels and establish consequences to enforce new habits. Don't lose your time searching for things in your home. When everything is where it's expected to be, calm replaces chaos. (If you're thinking, *I could do that if I had a bigger closet, more cupboards, or a housekeeper,* stay tuned for the next chapter, Baggage Check.)

Take a look at the hotbeds of entropy in your home. Where does disorder routinely occur? How can you create a system for tackling the gradual untidiness of these areas? Perhaps it's just a matter of designating and labeling specific storage containers. You may need to set a routine to keep infrequent tasks on the radar. Don't forget proper communication. For instance, if you keep an ongoing list of needed groceries and supplies, let everyone know to add to the list whatever commodities they finish.

For me, disorganization was found anywhere my children were. Now, I could have gone on picking up after them and telling myself, they're just kids, but instead I created a system for them to follow on their own. I gave them a hamper for their dirty clothes, a set of shelves specifically designated for their Legos, and a designated spot for their backpacks. The funny thing was, school had already introduced them to these types of systems. Starting as early as two-year-old day care, kids are taught to put the blocks in a certain bin and wash their hands before snack time. So it's natural to establish rules at home. It takes adult reasoning and effort to get these systems in place, but when they are clearly established and explained, children will follow them. It's actually a relief for children to have rules.

Open Spaces

During a three-year period in my childhood, my family moved into a house that was cavernous in relation to our possessions. Our living room was one of those typical, front-of-the-house rooms that no one used. The room had a couch, a loveseat and, in December, a decorated pine tree. The room was large enough for me to do four cartwheels diagonally across it. How do I know this? Because I was twelve, and that's what twelve-year-olds do when they have space to play. My brother was six at the time. He had a Dunk-It basketball net that was propped in front of one of the couches—and why not? No one ever sat in there. To my three siblings and me, this was the best place in the house. Part of me thinks my parents didn't mind either. We were safe and out of their hair, especially through those cold winter months; we could make a snowman in the yard or hula hoop in the living room. Ahh, the choices.

That house had a profound effect on the choices I made for my own house. I didn't buy an oversized house, but I did make sure the space I had was, at the very least, maneuverable and, at best, wide open.

At first, empty rooms were not a problem because we started out with barely any furniture. But after we started getting hand-me-downs and garbage picking, rooms began to fill up. It didn't seem like long before we were rearranging and resisting furniture. I wasn't going to allow stuff to close in on my (figurative) cartwheel space.

My dining room became that space—where I could walk freely. It was the designated do-all or do-nothing room. This was made possible by a secondhand stowaway dining room table, otherwise known as a drop-leaf table. The table came with only two chairs. That alone cut down on furniture in the room. When we pull out the table for large dinners with guests, we simply borrow the extra four chairs from our kitchen table—no need for the redundancy of extra chairs.

A drop-leaf table keeps my dining room open and free for use for any activity I choose.

For the most part, the table leaves are down, and the table remains up against the wall, giving way to maximum flow through the room. Now don't go thinking you can't have a wide-open dining room without a drop-leaf table. You could use a smaller table that doubles as a desk to create a dual purpose office-dining space. You could also tuck a card table behind a hutch and bring the table out for game night or crafting. The possibilities are end-less once you get past conforming to the traditional dining room with a commanding and space-consuming full dining room set.

Another awesome place to find open space is your garage. Let's imagine it without cars. What is left? My guess is a whole lot, from sports equip-ment to woodpiles to bikes, a picnic table, grill, and lawn mower. I could go on, right? What if this space could be useful as a woodworking studio or a place the kids could play on a rainy day? How would that change the way you live? Would you have a haven where you could create art projects? Or would it be a shared space where you could play around on Pinterest while

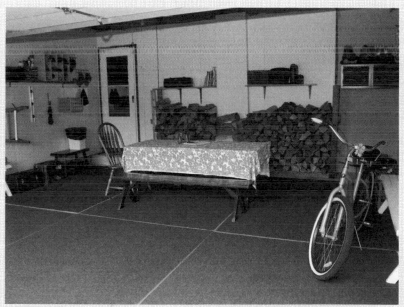

A clear garage can serve many functions for your family, including a play area, a hobby or craft space and a place to host summer parties.

the kiddos whack each other with pool noodles? (Hey, we all have our own ways to release tension.)

Don't sacrifice your garage space to your clutter. Take the leap and reduce what you have stored there. Create open space where you can park your car and engage in meaningful activities. My family uses the garage as an indoor-outdoor room in the summer. We put down indoor-outdoor carpet and park the car in the driveway. We host birthday parties there, play marathon games of Monopoly and share summer meals. It's a relaxing place where spills aren't a big deal and balls can get kicked around without a freak-out.

Think about the activities you can conduct at your house when you have the space to work with. It is gratifying to have the breathing room to accommodate personal interests on your own turf. Your home isn't just a storage unit for your possessions and a place to rest your head. It's the arena of your life. Your home holds the potential to host your creative and social functions when it is free from unmanaged consumption.

Reduce the Clutter in Your Schedule

Like all living creatures, humans were meant to be free. Freedom is movement. And the only way to move is to make room—in our lives and in our homes. Children typically have some free time in school (though this is be-

Exercise

This exercise will help you make the right decisions for your body, your time, and your space.

Sit in a room with no interruptions. Think about how your body feels. Do you need to plunge your face into a warm washcloth or turn on music? Look around the room. Do you like being there? Or is there a project you wish you could start or finish? Where do you feel your attention needs to go in order to most benefit you (and your immediate family, if applicable)?

Exercise

Chart your free-time activities for a week. Keep a daily free-time journal to log the activities, or inactivity you dedicated your free time to. In order for this to be effective, get a little obsessive about listing where you have spent your time. Your entries should include the activity plus the number of minutes spent on it.

At the end of the week, look back at your log and categorize your activities so you can make necessary adjustments. Do you need to set boundaries on reading social media updates, talking on the phone, or watching TV? If you had allotted more time to meal planning or updating your calendar, would it have saved you trips to the store or reduced the stress of rushing at the last minute?

Free time needs to be coordinated, just like other activities, so it can best be enjoyed.

coming shorter and shorter). But as adults, we typically fill up our free time with garbage or too many responsibilities.

When we've cleared our minds, rooms, and schedules, we find our creative selves. We're all born with creativity and purpose, but these qualities are stifled by obligations, clutter, visual information, and advertisements.

Look at us: We walk around getting pinged by our smartphones telling us what we should be doing. If we would listen to *ourselves*, we would know what we need and want to be doing.

Enough is Enough

Our free time is a battleground for boundaries. You might be thinking, *Free time? Who has time for that? I'm way too busy.* If you're too busy for free time, you need to evaluate your definition of the term and then establish boundaries.

We all have tasks we must do to continue functioning as healthy humans, but this list isn't as long as you think—grooming and hygiene, preparing and eating meals, sleeping, earning an income, and cleaning the house. Are all of these things done well in your life? If not, can you re-evaluate your schedule and make more time for them? When you give a task the proper amount of time it requires and then complete it in a timely manner, the stress related to the task generally melts away.

Part of the reason we don't have enough time to do these tasks is because we don't want to do them. Instead, we fill our schedules with other things that are more fun and, therefore, "relaxing." It's a myth that engaging in lots of fun activities reduces your stress. True, we all need to blow off some steam. But if you spend all of your time having fun, you'll eventually feel stress when your schedule doesn't accommodate the things you must do in order to function. When you don't get enough sleep because you stayed up watching television, the lack of sleep isn't the problem; watching too much television is.

Television, movies, the internet, books, socializing and going to parties and functions can rob you of so much time if you don't set boundaries. The easiest way to set boundaries is to say yes to what you really want and no to everything else. Watch only the TV programs and movies you really want to see. Limit yourself to thirty minutes online and stick to it (the Internet will be there tomorrow when you get back online). Accept invitations to

Find Your Own Meaning

Have you ever asked people what their plans were for Thanksgiving or Christmas? How many times did they list three or four households they were going to visit? When I asked a friend of mine what her family was doing on Christmas, she said, "We stay home. We spend the day putting toys together and playing." I almost died of envy. I can't say she had found the true meaning of Christmas, but she had found the true meaning of family. She and her husband have a clear picture of what is right for their family. Whatever your picture is, be sure you stay true to it. Don't chase someone else's picture.

parties and get-togethers only if you want to go. If you love to hang out with friends, limit your time to an hour or two instead of all evening. Remember, quantity doesn't always equal quality.

You might be wondering what you'll do with all that free time you have now that you're not parked in front of a screen or driving from one obligation to the next. The answer is, do whatever you want. I'm not here to tell you how to spend your free time after you start getting it back. (But odds are good that you have a list of things you would love to do, if you only had the time. You have the time—start tackling that list!) For now, it is important just to get your time back and be aware of how easily it's lost when you say yes to other people's schedules instead of your own.

Create Systems for Everyday Tasks

Eating and cleaning ourselves and our homes are everyday tasks we can't avoid. You have to do them, so why not do them as efficiently as possible? Write out your regular routine or plan for how you eat, bathe, and clean. How long does it take you to do this? If you're not sure, time yourself and record the steps as you do them. Then review the process to see how you can reduce time and effort.

Take your laundry routine, for instance. You may find it easier to do all of your laundry in a single day. A haphazard approach to tasks causes repeat work (rewashing forgotten clothes left in the washer for a day or two) and wasted time and resources (ironing wrinkled clothes left in the dryer). Block out the time you need so you can push through in a focused but relaxed manor.

Evaluate your grocery shopping plan and meal plans. You can involve the entire family in this task, from unloading the car and rotating expiration dates to deciding what goes in the freezer and what's on deck in the refrigerator for the next day's meals. The best time to ensure your food consumption is timed and prepped for maximizing freshness and reducing waste is right when the groceries enter your house. This is the best time to wash and cut up fresh fruit (assuming it's at peak ripeness). Take the time to assess your inventory and plan meals, if you haven't done so prior to shopping. A well-stocked pantry helps keep life moving smoothly and allows you to plan healthy meals. You'll be less tempted to eat out if you can whip up a meal at a moment's notice. In the summertime, grow your own organic garden. You'll have fresh veggies and fruit on tap all summer and often into fall. Keep an herb box in your kitchen to add fresh flavor to otherwise boring meals. It makes dishes interesting without going out of your way. I recommend taste-testing different herbs first and then growing only your favorites.

It seems so much easier to eat a microwave dinner in front of the TV than to cook an actual meal and sit at the table. But if you look deeper, you discover the truth—fresh, healthy meals are more nourishing and better for your body. And time spent with your family around the dinner table is more refreshing and engaging than anything on television. If you're out of practice, having a family dinner may take a while to get used to, but if you give it a chance, you likely won't want to go back.

> Take the time to plan how you'd like your things to be managed, your tasks to flow, and your time to be divided.

You can make mealtime much easier by employing one simple rule—everyone must try and eat new foods. My husband and I employ this rule in our house. We put a stop to accommodating picky eaters (myself included) and now save time and money by making one meal for the entire family. If you have young children, try sharing your entrée with them at restaurants instead of ordering junk food off the kid's menu. Having a broad palate also makes for an easier time when you're a guest in someone else's house. You won't need to pack and transport separate food, and when you get to your destination, you can help the hostess rather than fuss with your own menu ordeal.

Another time-saver is to designate eating areas in your home. This simple rule protects your furniture and eliminates crumbs and dirty dishes around your house. You won't have to scavenge the house for miscellaneous dishware and then soak and scrub off the hardened food.

Take the time to plan how you'd like your things to be managed, your tasks to flow and your time to be divided. Chunk your tasks and clutter into sequences and compartments so you can strategically organize your time and space. You'll thank yourself for the up-front initiative when you can find what you need when you need it and you effortlessly multitask through your housework.

Building Your Own Team

Extracurricular activities are often the biggest drain on a family's time. One organized sport can be a healthy part of childhood and adulthood. Being a part of a team teaches commitment, discipline, cooperation, physical fitness, and social skills. It's a great way to meet people and build friendships. The problem in today's society is that we rarely participate in only one thing. People get dry mouth just listing the activities and sports they have to run to. Meals are rushed, housework is neglected, and conversations are nonexistent. Parents drive to one neighboring town for a softball game and then back the same night for a soccer game. Parents complain, and often the children don't even want to be there. If this is the case, why are we doing this to ourselves? It's become an unnecessary waste of time.

Now I'm not telling you or your children to quit all your organized sports. I'm suggesting you evaluate the number of events you participate in and your reasons for participating and then weigh your options. Must you join a team or sign up for a class to practice or play the sport?

What ever happened to a pick-up game at the park? We lost ourselves in the fear of letting our kids do things at will. Everything has become organized and rigid. We've gone from one extreme to another. Several decades ago, we ran around until the streetlights came on. Today we have whiteboards in our kitchens outlining each day's events like a war strategy.

When my kids were in their early school years, my husband and I signed them up for swimming lessons. We spent eighty dollars to watch our boys sit next to the pool learning water safety for half the class. It was painful! My husband and I realized we could just as effectively teach our children to swim ourselves. We purchased a family membership to a local athletic center so we could swim as a family whenever there were open swims. The entire family participated, and the open swim schedule gave us a lot of flexibility in our schedule.

My oldest son and I are archers. It may seem like a tricky sport to practice because we live in suburbia, and at first it was. On Saturday mornings, I drove to the county north of us for lessons. There were days when my son would get carsick from the twenty-five-minute commute, and then he'd hardly want to participate once we got there. One day I looked around at the indoor archery range where we practiced. It was ten yards of open

Exercise

Create a three-column list to help evaluate your current schedule of extra-curricular activities.

In the first column, list any and all activities that you and your family participate in. In the second column, define the reasons you participate in each activity. In the last column, explore which activities you can eliminate and replace with easier, less expensive or less time-consuming alternatives. Is this something offered by your town instead of by a private club? Are there programs that don't require a minimum number of classes each week? Can you seek free instruction online instead of attending classes? Do you know someone who might have equipment you can purchase second-hand? Are there opportunities for carpooling?

space with vertical stacks of cardboard against the opposite wall. Ten yards is about the length of my basement! We spent an afternoon collecting free cardboard from a local bulk-membership store and set up an indoor range in our basement. Now we shoot our bows anytime we want and have reclaimed the time spent traveling and the money spent on lessons and gas.

We have a basketball hoop in our driveway and bikes in our garage. There are opportunities for recreation all around us. We don't need to scarf down Hot Pockets, fight traffic, have power struggles with coaches, or sit in the cold *watching* our kids. We play with our kids on our time, at our pace. And believe me, my kids meet other kids all over the neighborhood along the way.

Setting Boundaries

Now let's talk about those unnecessary responsibilities we fill our lives with. When it comes to taking control of your schedule, you need to put *yourself* in control of your time. Don't let others dictate how you spend *your* time. When I first started taking control of my time, instead of simply saying no, I would stumble when someone would ask me to do something that I didn't necessarily feel was a good use of my time. I am a terrible liar. I beat around the bush. I knew I couldn't accept the request, but in my painful and pro-longed way of saying no, I felt like I came off looking like:

a. a stick-in-the-mud outcast

b. a wife on a short leash

c. a rude bitch

d. a weirdo

Early in my marriage, my husband had the idea that he would write a list of ten excuses and attach them to the phone. That way when someone called and asked if we wanted to go to a spaghetti dinner at their church, I would be able to smoothly apologize and say that we had dinner plans at a friend's house. Next call: Shoot, I'd love to spend half my weekend winery hopping in a limo, but our sump pump gave out and I'm in the middle of clearing out my basement. Yes, those excuses were a sham, but I didn't know how to confidently say no without seeming rude or making the other person feel rejected. The problem is, an excuse is a one-time deal, and outside forces are consistent and persistent. They want *you* on *their* schedule. Logically, my sump pump wasn't going to have a bad day every time someone called, even though that was baloney to begin with. I had to set boundaries and be honest about them. The list of excuses by the phone never materialized because I knew ten excuses were not going to hold back the endless pressures of the outside world.

Unpredictability is a quality I'm not thrilled to discover in people. (This is not to be confused with spontaneity. You can be spontaneous while still being predictable.) I like to know what makes people tick; it's part of really knowing someone. That's why I feel it's only fair that I let the people around me know why I choose to spend my time the way I do. I'm not trying to tie it on the end of their nose; I just want to be honest. I want them to know, for instance, that purse parties aren't my thing. So if I get invited to one, I would decline by saying something like, "Thanks for the invite, but I'm really not a big fan of those types of events. I love to spend my time creating my own handbags and adding custom embroidery. Hey, if there is an extra catalog, I wouldn't mind taking a peek, just for ideas."

My response is polite and honest, and it leaves no open ends. I laid it on the line—this is who I am and what I do. I set expectations regarding my involvement up front. Notice I didn't say, "I would love to, but…" Why?

Because that's a lie, and it leaves me open to future invites that I would rather avoid. I would not love to go to the party, but saying that gives the person the impression that she should invite me again the next time a similar event comes around. Being direct closes that door. If someone does, by chance, invite you to another party, you can feel confident using the same response. You are being predictable in your response. You can use this approach for anything you are asked to do.

I'm honest to those around me, but most important, I'm honest to myself and my values. The activities my family and I participate in need to be sensibly justified. It isn't that I'm automatically going to say "no way" to every invitation or offer I receive. I simply pause to ask myself a few questions before I answer:

a. Do I want to say yes because I'll feel guilty or embarrassed if I say no?
b. Do I want to accept because I'm bored?
c. Is it a lifestyle standard? Is it easier to sign up than explore alternatives?
d. Will I feel sorry for myself if I don't? Will I feel like I'm the only one who didn't...?

If I answer yes to these questions, I know I'm not doing it for the right reasons, and I'll probably be happier saying no to the offer. It may look like I'm saying no all the time, but every time I say no to someone else, I say yes to myself and my priorities.

The Guilt Trip

I went to Catholic schools for thirteen years. Needless to say, guilt has been ingrained into my brain. It's terrible. You don't want to let people down, hurt their feelings, or feel like a jerk. But at what point do we realize that our own desires are being suppressed because we're doing what other people want? The Reduction Rebel is nobody's fool. We are on our own path with our own goals and values. But in order to forge ahead on the path, we must understand how to keep our decision making from turning to Jell-O in the face of guilt.

When we subscribe to outside influences on our time and money, eventually the guilt falls on what we're not doing. We become guilty, stressed, or perhaps even angry that we've followed someone else's lead or suggestion and were not true to our own desires, values, and talents.

Calling All Rebels

There is no question that fending off and circumventing invitations that don't align with your Reduction Rebel lifestyle can be a drag, so your real goal is to find like-minded rebels. For starters, don't dump your current friends because they are not Reduction Rebels. Who says they're not going to welcome the idea? Chances are, when your friends see the changes in your life, they're going to be interested in how you arrived at the new you. Sometimes people need to see the reduction results to become believers. Share your experiences, and your friends may end up joining you.

In your community, keep in mind that compliments are windows to the soul as well. If you see someone wearing an individualistic piece of jewelry, tell that person how much you like it. There is bound to be a personal story behind it. Start to take notice of details. My son brought home a handmade Valentine one year, and I asked who gave it to him. Later that year I was put on a committee with the student's mother, and I had a built-in conversation starter.

Although Reduction Rebels may not wear their personal manifesto on their sleeve, if they enjoy what they are doing, they'll be open about it when you ask the right questions. Nothing tests the waters like simple get-to-know-you questions like, "Have you ever been on (insert a popular website that you frequent)?" Even if they haven't heard of the site, you'll be able to gauge their interest in the topic.

And, of course, the internet is a great way to connect with like-minded people. When my free time opened up and I was looking for other crafty up-cyclers, I joined a group of recycle artists through Meetup.com. That site is a smorgasbord of groups that cater to all sorts of unique interests. You may share hobbies with people in your social network circle. Browse through their posts and maybe you'll find events they've organized or attended where your passions would fit right in.

There's nothing like swapping trade secrets with people who are equally interested in the hobbies you enjoy, whether it's gardening, sewing, woodworking, couponing, or hiking.

Reduce the Clutter in Your Spending Habits

I want to be clear about exactly where I'm coming from—the big picture stuff. The original goal in my family's reduction lifestyle was to free up our time so we could reduce our stress. The best way for us to free up time was to go to one income. But with all of our debt, going down to one income seemed like a pretty crazy, impossible thing to do. So our intermediate goal became to be completely debt-free—no mortgage, no car payment, no student loans. We wanted a crystal-clear financial slate with a well-padded emergency fund. On the traditional plan, this feat would normally take thirty years. It took us less than seven years.

We trimmed a lot of fat.

We'd bought a house, our first child was on the way, and our furniture situation looked, well, like we'd been robbed. We were just starting out and on a path of one-time purchases. I remember going to some store and walking out with one hundred dollars worth of trash cans for around the house—we're talking about basic, white plastic trash cans. We didn't even get stainless steel ones with the foot pedal that pops the top open. One hundred bucks on trash cans; I was flipping out.

I more vividly remember the night we took our newborn to the Galleria Mall and looked through Bombay and Pottery Barn for home furnishings.

The Reduction Rebel's spending motto: why spend money when you don't have to?

We didn't buy a thing. On the way home we passed a pile of garbage on the side of the road. In it was a large, framed painting. Now I'm not going to knock your pants off and tell you it was an original painting from the sixteenth century. All I can say is that after some spray paint to the frame and delicate hand painting on the mat, it's been hanging in our living room for nine years. This pick wasn't exceptional, but it taught me something that led me to the Reduction Rebel's spending motto: Why spend money when you don't have to? My husband and I knew that once a week, in every neighborhood, there were going to be piles of "garbage" where we could hit pay dirt again.

Free furniture and basic repair skills became financial game-changers for us, which is why a good portion of this book is dedicated to those subjects. But that's not all that goes into being a Reduction Rebel. We have applied our resourcefulness to all aspects of our retail life.

This is not a get-it-on-the-cheap approach. We are not maniacs with coupon binders. That lifestyle may reduce cost, but it in no way reduces production, consumption, time, and clutter. We save money by limiting our intake, enjoying what nature already provides and using our skills and common sense to make do with what we already have.

Different Isn't Sexy

In my twenties, I was really into distance bicycle riding. I completed three cross-state rides, a century, and a bunch of other fund-raising rides. Throughout the thousands of miles I biked, I never bought any gear to enhance my performance. Most often I was the only rider without a road bike. Yes, I just used the mountain bike I bought on sale and swapped out the tires. I knew me. Even though biking was a serious hobby, it wasn't like I was participating in the Tour de France. I biked because I enjoyed the experience, not for glory or fame or cutting-edge equipment. All the same, I stuck out like a sore thumb.

When my friend and I did a week-long ride down the coast of California, we were in the company of some older, die-hard riders. During the shuttle ride from the airport to the starting point, they were chatting with us about their name-brand equipment. They were throwing out big names and wanted to know what we had. Finally my friend cut the guy off, exclaiming, "We don't get geeked out." I'll never forget it. I was so proud of her for standing up against ridiculous status symbols. The next morning, we showed up for breakfast in our camisoles; the other riders were sporting spandex from shoulder to mid thigh. While waiting in the Johnny-on-the-Spot line, I dropped my helmet on the pavement. The woman behind me looked down and literally gasped, "You forgot your riding shoes!" She said it as if I were in bare feet. I was wearing an old pair of sandals. The soles were worn just enough that they fit snuggly in my toe clips. These sandals were seriously comfortable, like all well-worn shoes. Why would I need to buy special shoes just to push bike pedals?

"These are my riding shoes," I said confidently.

What makes you happier: living according to your values, or receiving acceptance and approval from society? People's threshold for accepting what is different fluctuates on the premise of culture, religion, upbringing,

Entertainment by Nature

Here are some Reduction Rebel-approved activities that lend themselves to learning opportunities, family time, and consumption control:

EXPERIENCE	CREATE
Take a hike	Design and whittle a walking stick
Go bird watching	Make a birdfeeder or birdbath
Collect rocks	Paint rocks; make domino rocks
Hunt for sea glass	Make jewelry or a mosaic
Visit different playgrounds	Build a broom-handle tree swing
Star gaze	Make flashlight slides of constellations
Fly a kite	Make your own kite
Play nature bingo or have a nature scavenger hunt	Construct a sculpture from found items in nature

and personality. So why aren't we more accepting of differences when it comes to money? Everyone wants to appear to have money, whether they do or not. Society tells us that to keep up and be your best, you have to have the newest, the latest and the best things and shop at the hottest, trendiest, and most exclusive stores. This is how you earn and keep respect. Facebook, American Girl, iTunes—it's all part of the criteria. And if you don't keep up with society, you're out. Friends of mine have explained to me that their kids have to be on Facebook or the kids won't be invited to parties. Eleven-year-olds are hosting parties?

The truth is, you don't have to keep up to be happy. I still enjoyed my California bike ride, despite not having professional equipment (and the

After years of collecting rocks from ponds, beaches, woods, and the side of the road, they provide a walking tour of our travels as well as curb appeal. Let your nature hobbies have a positive effect on your home.

money I saved by not buying the equipment helped pay for the trip). Yes, other people may not appreciate your style or understand your values, and yes, they may judge you and even think you're (gasp) cheap, but we all know that at the end of the day, peace of mind and financial security are far more important than social status and the opinions of strangers or casual acquaintances. To live as a Reduction Rebel means sometimes you just have to be cool with being on the outs.

Here We Are, Now Entertain Us

As human beings, we need and desire new experiences to help stimulate and foster our mental and emotional well-being. A simpler way to say it

Low-Cost Entertainment

As a Reduction Rebel, your goal is to change your consumption habits, but as a human being, you desire to have friends. How do you engage in social activities without compromising your reduction principles? Try these alternatives:

The benefits to the suggestions in the following chart go beyond saving money and maximizing your free time. They provide creative stimulation (aka, brain activity), mind enrichment, and opportunities for real human connections. You'll notice a real spark in someone's enthusiasm when you give that person an opportunity to express herself, too. You get to know a person much better when you allow for creative synergy in your time together. Think about times when you've initiated a group activity or worked on a committee where you helped plan an event or rally around a cause. By engaging in your interests and surrounding yourself with fellow enthusiasts, you learn from one another and become powerful resources of information and companionship.

is, we need to be entertained. What's the first activity you think of when you're asked to go out for the evening? It's likely eating at a restaurant or watching a movie.

People have become so used to going out to eat that it simply becomes entertainment. In reality, this "fun" costs a lot of time and money and it's typically not healthy. In one meal, you're spending enough money to feed your family for a week. Assess the comparison. You are trading twenty meals for one meal. That fleeting one-and-a-half-hour outing offsets six-and-half days worth of your food budget. Was the experience really that rewarding?

The truth is, you can find far more stimulating forms of entertainment for free. Simply enjoy what's around you and use your creativity. If you enjoy sharing meals with people, invite them to your home for dinner. You can try new dishes and cooking techniques.

YOU'RE ASKED TO	REDUCTION REBEL ALTERNATIVE SUGGESTION
Go to the movies or bowling	Rent a movie from the library or RedBox; play charades; have game night
Sign up for a fitness class	Organize a walking date; play tennis at the local courts
Come over to watch the game	Call some friends for volleyball in the yard; take the kids to a playground and bring the Frisbee for the adults
Try out a new restaurant	Host a chili cook-off
Visit a museum	Browse flea markets or barn sales; take a nature hike
Have a spa day	Likely you already have the ingredients for a spa treatment right in your own kitchen: coffee grounds, tea bags, oranges, cucumbers, and egg whites
Ride horses; shoot paintballs	Go for it! There's nothing wrong with trying something new every once in a great while. This is what makes it special.

Don't Do the Money Match

The UK has done some interesting studies on overconsumption, leading to statistics like four out of five people receive gifts they don't want. Three percent of those ungrateful recipients throw their unwanted gifts directly into the trash. What would you do if you knew someone threw out the gift you just spent money on? I would cry and opt for a gift card next time. I'd save on shipping, wrapping, lugging, and potential landfill fodder.

Now, it's human nature to reciprocate. When someone does something kind for us, we want to do something kind in return. But we do not need to feel obligated to match other people's extravagance. We should definitely appreciate what others have shared with us, but please don't let someone else's choices emotionally influence your purchases.

Exercise

Who has you making recurring appointments? Is it your chiropractor? The piano tuner? Does the dry cleaner come by every Tuesday, so you feel obligated to dig up something that needs to be cleaned?

Take a look at the pace at which you are revisiting service providers. You may find you don't need them nearly as often, or even at all.

If your friends have you over for lobster and brandy, that's their choice. There is nothing wrong with having them over for grilled spinach-and-artichoke pizza paired with fresh-squeezed lemonade.

Here's another scenario: Your kids have been invited to several birthday parties throughout the year. Each party has been at an entertainment facility (go-karts, bounce houses, laser tag). Now it's your son's birthday. You may be thinking, *How am I going to have these people in my backyard eating Popsicles and shooting squirt guns? They spent hundreds of dollars and now I'm going to turn around and spend thirty dollars.* The answer is, these are kids. They've never met a scavenger hunt or a water balloon toss they didn't like. It's okay to allow them to have an imagination instead of a pony. This is where we create! It's an awesome thing.

Routine Expenditures

My good friend is a hairdresser, and I am her worst client. The last time I went to get my haircut, she let me know that it was the first time I was getting my hair cut in a year. I wasn't even fully through the salon door when she said this. My reaction could easily have been guilt or embarrassment. I could have apologized, but honestly, my next appointment will likely be in a year from now. My first thought was, "Wow, I'm still getting compliments on my hair." I eat healthy and shower daily. I like the way my hair looks. Do I really need to get my ends trimmed every six weeks?

Last summer I set out to lower or eliminate my cable bill. After all, alternatives such as satellite and online streaming sites, are sending buckshot into the would-be monopoly of the cable industry. So after doing the research, I still felt cable was the best option for us. This didn't mean, however, that I was going to render myself complacent. I was still going to see if I could do something about my cable bill. I called. I got stiff-armed. My next move was to make an appointment with a cable competitor. This wasn't a big deal, except the competitor required a credit check.

Now, I wasn't all bluff. I simply let the cable company know I was switching television and internet providers, and based on the price they quoted me for phone service, I'd make a decision on where I was going for that. This tactic worked. They instantly knocked twenty-six dollars off my monthly bill. That was a 312-dollar savings. Nothing changed on my service except the cost. I did the same thing for my parents' cable bill. When the customer service rep started to resist my request for a price break, she noted that my parents had been customers since 1972 and backed down. It's about time we looked at bills that are being sent out every month for upward of forty years.

Another routine expense people take on is the gym. They get on the monthly membership cycle, plus pay extra for classes. It becomes another thing they feel guilted into doing: *I paid, therefore I have to pull myself out of bed before work to go. Or, put the kids to bed and miss out on quiet time with my spouse so I can justify this expense in my life.* It's another obligation in your schedule and another payment. The truth is, the average American is not a fitness

Exercise

Reverse the roles of coach and student—have your kids be your personal trainer. School-age children attend physical education class at least once a week. Ask them to show you some new drills. See how being in charge makes your children feel.

Don't have kids? Take turns with your friends being fitness instructors. The planning and creativity is half the fun—or 75 percent of the fun. Just saying.

Protect Your Credit

Every time a company, landlord, lender or potential employer checks your credit report, it can marginally lower your score. Some creditors view repeated credit checks as a negative indication of your financial situation because you could be over extending yourself with multiple loans. Over time, continual checks will lower your score. It's a necessary evil, but when possible, opt to avoid such procedures.

buff. Ask any doctor, and they'll tell you to go take a walk. It's free. You're not going to get injured. And best of all, you can talk to a friend, a loved one, or your child while you do it.

Higher Goals

Being a Reduction Rebel doesn't mean you never spend any money and you always put up with secondhand things. It's not about living the life of a pauper or a miser.

Rather, a Reduction Rebel understands what he or she truly wants in life and then uses all available resources—time, creativity, and money—to pursue it. In other words, Reduction Rebels are realistic about what they have and make sacrifices in areas that don't matter as much to them so they are free to fully explore and enjoy their passions. I won't tell you what to spend your time and money on. That's for you to decide. It's your life. You know what's best for you, and you best understand what sacrifices you are willing to make.

I don't have a second car or a cell phone. I wear used clothes and once garbage-picked a can of corn. But I have a thousand-dollar camera. Why do I do this? The answer is simple. I understand what I really want and need. I'm realistic. I know I can't have both a designer handbag and a high-end camera. I'd rather have a high-end camera than brand-new clothes. And because of this, I am able to achieve my goals and not end up distracted by what everyone else has and wants.

The point is, contrary to what advertisers would have us believe, very few of us can afford to have it all. Reduction Rebels understand that and, therefore, decide to go after the best they can afford of what they really want, often making other sacrifices to achieve the goal.

Maybe you value fashion, and the latest trendy clothing brings you great joy. There's nothing wrong with that. Set a budget you can live with and find ways to enhance your clothing budget. Maybe you skip coffee each week, or you sell two old pieces online or through consignment and use the funds for a new piece. Make it work for you.

The easiest way to reach your higher goals—whether it's being debt-free or buying a new car or making a high-end purchase for a hobby—is to curb your everyday consumption. A cup of coffee is only three dollars. Those T-shirts were on sale two for twenty dollars. These are small, no-brainer purchases we often make because the amount seems so inconsequential. But small expenses snowball. A three-dollar cup of coffee each day or twenty-dollar purchase each week adds up to more than a thousand dollars a year! These small purchases bring little gratification and often end up in the trash.

I know a family who is part of the 25 percent of Americans who own a two-car garage, yet cannot fit their cars in it because the garage is filled with other stuff. One day I was standing in their driveway with the husband. In exasperation, he looked at the piles of junk and said, "I'd love to rent a Dumpster and invite my mother-in-law over. As all this stuff is being shoved into the Dumpster, I'd like to say to her, 'There goes your retirement fund.'" I could feel his pain. His situation had gotten out of control. But, I have to say, the antidote is tough love.

Reduction Rebels forgo all the little stuff so they can focus on finding items truly worthy of their money and time. We know what's out there, and for goodness sake, the little stuff will not distract us.

It feels great to rally your talents and wrangle your burdens to clear a path toward your true passions. You experience abundant fulfillment when a sense of purpose brings order, stress relief, and clarity to your schedule and surroundings. This sense of purpose will help guide your daily decisions and long-term goals. And this culmination of positive decisions will yield a lifestyle that gives you control of your money, possessions, home, and free time.

3: Baggage Check

Fourteen years ago, I had to purchase a renter's insurance policy after my cat bit the mailman. I had nothing of value in my apartment; seriously, I was a baby step out of college and borderline transient. I just needed to cover my feline liability. The insurance agent interrogated me on the value of my personal property. I'll never forget him saying, "Come on, every woman is either into shoes, sweaters, purses, or earrings."

Every woman? This guy was pretty presumptuous! But maybe he was right; every person does tend to indulge in one thing or another. And somewhere along the timeline of American culture, our hierarchy of needs—food, clothing, and shelter—got perverted.

Do we need nineteen pairs of shoes, three hundred television channels, and four cars in the driveway? Do we even need two cars in the driveway?

We are masters at collecting. We buy big, beautiful homes for storing all our stuff. At every birthday, holiday, hurt feeling, promotion, impulse, and killer sale, we bring more stuff into our homes. Seasons change, weight fluctuates, interests fade, and we're back at the checkout counter where we exchange our money to fulfill status, curiosity, and boredom.

> We are masters at collecting... At every birthday, holiday, hurt feeling, promotion, impulse, and killer sale, we bring more stuff into our homes.

This chapter will help you put your consumer habits into perspective so you buy less and savor what you do have more. Consuming less also means less clutter in your home that will eventually end up in the landfill.

When a Deal Isn't a Deal

I'm all about purchasing something for the best possible price. If you buy something at store A for less than what you would have paid at store B, you've made a wise purchase. This is the groundwork for being a conscious consumer. You are deciding what you need and where you're buying it. You're trying to get the best quality for the best price for exactly what you need. But there's a difference between purchasing something for a good price and purchasing something simply because it is a good price.

In recent years, consumer product companies have increased their in-store advertising by 25 percent. They offer an amazing deal on a product or two to lure you into the store, and as soon as you're in, you're vulnerable. Just look at Black Friday deals. People line up for the chance to spend money, and even if they aren't one of the lucky few who manage to get the deal, they likely don't leave the store empty-handed. They find something to buy. I've been there—feeling awkward going into a store and not buying something. Sometimes we are even detoured to walk through the checkout lanes to get out of the store. Wait, have one last look at candy, batteries, and magazines before you go.

Advertisements say, "Come in and save!" Those four words should not be put together, but we fall for it every time. We allow ourselves to feel desperate, as if the opportunity or price will no longer be available if we don't act now. Sure, you don't need a new shirt, let alone two, but it's buy one, get one free. You'd be crazy to miss out on the savings, right?

This is the type of mindless, manipulative consumerism that draws us into spending money we don't have on things we don't need. We're not making a calculated decision about something we need; we're just reacting to the numbers: 20 percent off, two for one, mail-in rebate (which is just another way for a company to collect your personal information for marketing and advertising purposes). Because a discount can be sizable, we automatically think that's going to be the best deal.

When I was a kid, my father worked for General Motors. He bought a new car because he could get the GM employee discount. My parents had very little money, so the car they bought was a Chevy Citation. We were a family of six in a car made for four. My mother had to sit in the back seat, and my brother and I shared the front passenger seat with the seatbelt stretched across the two of us. I hope you're either crying or doubled over laughing at this ridiculous situation. Why wouldn't they buy a used station wagon? Because my dad wouldn't have been able to use his employee discount. The manufacturer and dealer really made out in this deal. My parents still spent more than they needed to spend for something that didn't meet their needs.

> Good spending decisions are made when we know we're spending money, not fooled into thinking we're saving money.

When we buy something based on manufactured opportunity and a seller's suggestions, we are spending money and not saving it. Even if you still have money left in your pocket after the purchase, you still have less money than before.

Good spending decisions are made when we know we're spending money, not fooled into thinking we're saving money. Give yourself permission to miss a sale. Don't go shopping if you don't need something. When

Exercise

Are you savvy enough to get an entire outfit plus accessories for less than forty dollars? Take the family or plan a girlfriend outing to a local consignment shop. Buy local, recycle, and feel the exhilaration of treasure hunting.

you need to make a purchase, decide how much you are willing to spend on the item and then shop around for the best price. If you can't find anything in your price range, have patience and wait for a sale, or look for a used item you can afford.

Used is Still New to You

Part of changing your consumption habits is realizing that malls, department stores, and big-box stores aren't the only places you can find items you need. In many cases, you can find a used version of what you need for a fraction of the cost, or even free. The reality of opportunity costs helped motivate my husband and me to garbage-pick more than half the furniture in our house. If you can't find it at the curb, check out the free listings on Craigslist or Freecycle.org. Don't think that because it came from the curb, my husband and I settled for whatever we could find and brought home trash. We were selective and chose items we knew we could fix up and use.

> Picking something up just because it's free is just as bad as buying something just because it's on sale... If you don't need it, don't bring it into your life.

Picking something up just because it's free is just as bad as buying something just because it's on sale. It will become useless clutter in your home. If you don't need it, don't bring it into your life.

All of my kids' clothing, shoes included, are purchased at consignment shops. I get geeked buying Gap pants for four dollars and Sperry loafers for eight dollars. I even got myself a Lilly Pulitzer skirt for two dollars at a consignment shop. (Sorry, I'm kind of bragging, but I'm telling you this to prove that you can have nice things at a fraction of the cost. If I can do it, so can you.) And the clothes that are in good shape when we're done with them go back to the consignment shop to be sold. If you have a consignment shop or two that you frequent, make sure you get on their e-mail list. They'll let you know when you can get shirts for seventy-five cents, unlike retail shops that let you know when you can get a measly seventy-five cents off. You'll also see a pattern as to when consignment shops have sales, usually around holidays. So if you need something and it's a couple weeks until Easter, you'll know to wait for the sale to get anything in the store at 25 to 75 percent off.

I'm a huge fan of Craigslist because you can search for specific things you're looking for and it's local, so there's no shipping involved. As a seller, there is no cost to post an unlimited number of items for sale. Another great local resource is your weekly newspaper. These papers are usually free at the library or coffee shops. Typically, they have a classifieds section for items under one hundred dollars. These classified ads are free to the seller. So if someone wants to sell a bike, golf clubs, baby gear—you name it—they'll sell it for under a hundred dollars in the paper so they don't have to pay for the ad. In other words, a crib that might sell on Craigslist for 175 dollars, will go in the paper for ninety-nine dollars so there is no cost to the seller.

Our money goes further when we're on the hunt—online, at second-hand outlets and especially at the curb.

This House is Not a Suitcase

In the contest between spending and saving, too often the bank account loses, and we bring home our "trophies" to pile up in our closets, basements, and kitchen cabinets.

Our closets devolve into avalanches, and our kitchen counters look like rummage sales. Bags of plastic toys sit in baskets around the house. A new toilet seat sits in its package, endlessly waiting to replace the old one. The banister cannot be seen under the multitude of coats flung upon it. The attic is no longer approachable, and even the car has become a moving self-storage unit.

So many people who've purchased stuff from me on Craigslist arrive at my house with a vehicle that is already full. They have to rearrange an air compressor, skateboard, set of golf clubs, leaf blower, lounge chairs, box of books—you name it—to make room for their latest treasure. They leave with a mirror sticking out of their sunroof. I wonder, if they can barely fit something in their car, do they even have room for it in their house?

We are all hoarders to some degree. We're masters of collecting. When the garage is full, we buy a shed. Our cars no longer fit in the garage, so we add a carport. The dining room table is covered, so we eat out with friends instead of having them over for dinner. Have you ever changed your mind about hosting a get-together because you couldn't get your house present-able for guests? Has your laptop found a spot in the living room because your home office is a necropolis for unused exercise equipment, outdat-ed media products and forgotten projects? We need stuff management. Whether it's in our house or driveway, our stuff needs to be managed.

We accumulated all this stuff because we thought it would either make our lives easier or bring us joy. We don't realize that part of the stress we feel is caused by the excess in our lives. Our possessions are dictating our free time. Sundays used to be for relaxing and eating, and now they're spent cleaning the garage. When we clean the ga-rage, what do we do? We wheel everything out. Someone walks by and asks if we're having a sale. We politely say no, and then make a face like, "What's their problem?" We blow out the dirt and leaves, and return ev-erything to the garage in orderly rows. We'll need to clean it again in a couple weeks, but by then we'll be busy weed whacking around the swing set, trampoline, birdbath, and sandbox. We'll be vacuuming the pool and exterminating the beehive in the tree house. Think about what we're doing.

> Our possessions are dictating our free time. Sundays used to be for relaxing and eating, and now they're spent cleaning the garage.

We spend all this time maintaining what we bought. Instead of enjoy-ing a select few things that we're really excited about, like a tennis enthusi-ast restringing a racquet, we have one thing after another to look after. Soon we're just going through the motions, checking things off our to-do lists. We don't even consider why we have something or the possibility that we could free ourselves from the maintenance by getting rid of it. Do you ever think about how often you use the thing you're maintaining?

Why do you have a twenty-four-foot boat, worth fifteen grand, taking up half your driveway when you took it out only once last year? Why do you have a convertible in storage when you didn't drive it last year? Do you know anyone who has rented storage units, to the tune of thousands of dollars, for useless things they were afraid of losing? That is an expensive emotional attachment! Regardless of where it's being stored (or what it costs or is worth), we all have small things, and some very large things, that we don't use. Start your reduction plan with the large things and work your way down to the small things. It's liberating.

You may not have a boat or spare sports car in your driveway, but have you ever looked at what percentage your car payment is to your mortgage? When my family made this assessment, we found our car was costing us half of our monthly mortgage payment. So for one price you get a car, double the price and you get a whole house. Stack up your home against having a second car. Has transportation joined the ranks of food, clothing, and shelter? For my family, owning a second car did not make sense in our hierarchy of needs. A second car was a very expensive luxury. This was our assessment. My husband and I were able to get rid of the car because when our first son was born, we decided that I would be a stay-at-home mom. That lasted seven months until I accepted a telecommuting job. Yes, working from home was my ticket to freedom from a second car and the payments, gas, and maintenance that comes with it. Too many people who know me can't see it that way. They think that without access to a car during the day, I'm trapped in suburbia. The truth is, I live within walking distance to a grocery store and a playground. What more could a mom need? I'm the parent who rides her bike to parent-teacher conferences and play dates. Honestly, it makes me feel youthful and patriotic.

In my twenties, I had a thirty-five-minute commute to work each morning, so I understand that sometimes a car is vital to your lifestyle. However, in the summer, I took the commuter train to the station closest to work and rode my bike the last two miles. Clearly this would not have worked if I had a child to take to day care or if public transportation wasn't available. I'm just saying it's an option, just like carpooling. My neighbor was spending ten dollars a day on gas going to the same place as another guy in our neighborhood. They networked and arranged a carpooling schedule. One of my former co-workers had a totally unreliable car. So instead of buying a backup car to use when his transmission went out or brakes failed, he'd call me to come get him. That worked, too. I know another couple that work for the same company and, therefore, are able to have one car. It can be done in many cases; you just need to look at the numbers instead of focusing on the convenience factor.

Getting rid of your second car may not work for you. I'm just asking that you look at the numbers. There may be a snowmobile, Jet Ski or ATV in your garage that you can part with for five thousand dollars, which you can use toward your mortgage. Or you may be able to sell back your current car and buy a much less expensive used car as a way to reduce your monthly payments. It isn't hard to do, especially when those payments are redirected into paying off the principle on your mortgage faster.

Be Okay With Good-Bye

Have you ever thought about getting rid of stuff to avoid the hassle of it altogether? I'm sure you have, but you probably haven't acted on that thought, have you? The truth is, getting rid of stuff is easier said than done. We tell ourselves that we can't part with something because we paid a lot of money

Exercise

Evaluate the contents of each room in your home and ask yourself:

1. Do I even need this?
2. Has this been used in the last year?
3. Do I own something else that serves the same purpose? (i.e., the Magic Bullet and a blender)
4. Am I hanging on to something that could be used and enjoyed by someone else?
5. Is this costing me money or space that I don't have?

If you answer no to questions 1 and 2 and yes to questions 3–5, why are you keeping the item? Give yourself permission to let it go.

for it. We can't give it away because we haven't worn it yet—or there's a chance we might wear it to some unknown event in the future.

For the longest time, I had two sewing machines. One I used, and the other sat on the floor of my office closet like an anvil. It was in the way, but I was afraid something might happen to my main sewing machine, so I had to keep the other one, just in case. I might as well have towed a spare car around in case I had a breakdown. But my spare was a 1965 Pfaff sewing machine that worked perfectly. How would I find another one, I reasoned. Who cares! The problem didn't exist; it was hypothetical. Can you imagine what a house would look like if there were a backup refrigerator in the garage and a backup stove in the basement next to the backup washing machine? Why don't you just buy a backup house in case yours gets flooded? Whether it's a backup or not, if you're not using it, it's time to get rid of it. It's not enhancing your life; it's taking away from your life. Things that we are needlessly attached to take a bit of our freedom, and they could be enhancing someone else's life.

All the clothes and toys that your kids have outgrown are taking up space; they're not preserving their youth. After I sold my sons' Power Wheels riding toys, I ran in the house and sobbed. I couldn't stand the thought of them not riding them around the yard all summer. Those vehicles marked their toddler years. I was saying good-bye to their smiling faces, waving as they passed by me, trick-or-treating with their candy-filled pumpkins in the trunk. Oh, it hurt. It hurt badly—for maybe five minutes. I realized that for my sons, the era of the toys had already passed. They were too big to use them. Holding on to them for several more years wouldn't change the fact that they were growing up. They wouldn't ride them again, whether we kept them or not. By getting rid of them right away, I was able to sell the toys for a decent price. If I'd held on to them and let them depreciate in useless nostalgia, they would have been thrown away years in the future. That's a waste of resources, opportunities, and space. Another family got to enjoy them while we moved on. By the end of the week, my husband had used the money from the sale to start an investment portfolio for the kids. We were able to use the money from the sale to fund something greater. Moving on also meant that the kids were going to start riding bikes. The garage has two little bikes in it now. We can get excited once again to see them teeter along the sidewalk as they find their inner balance on two wheels. Power Wheels weren't the end of their riding days; they had graduated to bicycles. In all areas of life, we need to graduate to better things and let go of the old things.

Memories do not need to come in a tangible form. You had a great time playing darts in college; I get it. But keeping the dartboard in your basement will not help you relive the fun. There are current college students who'd love to pick up that dartboard for their apartment at a fraction of the retail cost. You had your time; now they have theirs. It feels good. And they'll appreciate it. It's relevant to their current lifestyle and not just an icon of the past. The same can be said for things like motorcycle jackets, paintball guns, and video game players. My brother gave my kids his PlayStation that is way more than a decade out of date but still relevant to a six- and four-year-old. He wasn't using it, and his son was an infant at the time. Instantly, he was my kid's hero. He felt like a million bucks; the gray box was out of his entertainment center, and my kids had a new, free toy. Not only that, we were able to pick up extra games for a few dollars at a secondhand gaming shop.

I'm not asking you to part with your grandmother's needlework or family heirloom just to make some cash. I'm saying, ask the questions. If it's been sitting around your house for a year and you're not using it, it's a good indication that you don't need it. Assess true clutter issues, like what is keeping your linen closet from fully closing.

Eliminate Redundancies

After you have gone through the clutter, you're going to hit the redundancies. This can be a simple analysis like, "I have two curio cabinets. Let's get rid of one." The real challenge is to work your way into the nitty-gritty of your possessions, not just the obvious, like fourteen baseball caps or fifty pairs of earrings. Make sure you're looking at the numbers. When we compared our cell phone cost to what the cable company was offering, we realized we could get cable, Internet, and digital phone for the same monthly cost as our cell phone. Because we'd eliminated the second car, I was typically home

How to Throw a Barter Party

In honor of the growing awareness of overconsumerism and green initiatives, these types of "barties" (also called a swap or swish) are becoming more popular.

1. Pick a specific genre. Popular themes are gently used toys, clothes, books, household items, or holiday gifts that have found their way to a dark corner—basically anything that is giftable, which automatically disqualifies things like underwear, paper clips, and broken appliances. Don't forget nontangible things like services; for example, I'll till your garden if you walk my dog while I'm on vacation. Pick a theme that is relevant to the people you'll be inviting; for example, if it's a toy or children's clothing swap, you wouldn't want to invite childless friends and family.

2. Invite your family and friends via social media, e-vites, or traditional snail mail, whatever works for you and your group. If you're hosting a party at your house, six to ten guests is usually an appropriate number.

3. Each guest receives a poker chip for each item or service IOU he or she brings. Guests then can use their poker chips to "buy" something that another guest brought. Win, win! Some people assign values to the items coming in—a cashmere sweater gets five chips and a cotton skirt gets two, but this can create a lot more work. I recommend keeping it to simple one-to-one trades.

If anything is left over, it can go up for grabs or be donated—current owner's choice.

when my husband was at work. When we had a company cell phone, we used it mostly for idle chatting as we drove around. Yeah, it was convenient for ordering food when we were out, but was that convenience worth 150 dollars a month? There was a phone at home and at my husband's work, so we didn't need another phone.

People often carry cell phones in case of emergencies. If there is an emergency, you can be paged at work or reached at home. If you're running errands, it's not like you're going to be away from all telephone access for a substantial stretch of time where you couldn't check your messages if you needed to. It's not like I'm hiking in remote Utah or lost amid gang warfare in Guatemala City. In a pinch, I can always ask to use someone else's phone. A perfect example of this came when my husband got into a car accident. When he safely emerged from the wreckage formerly known as our only car, the other drivers involved had their phones to call the police. When the police arrived, my husband used their phone, and the officer ended up giving my husband a ride home, too.

The Cost of Convenience

It may seem easy to store six bikes in your garage, anticipating your kids will grow into your old bikes. The same is true with keeping your wedding dress, which is the size of a phone booth, in your closet. You may have two hundred pictures of you wearing the dress and no plans to wear it again, yet you hold on to it physically and emotionally. These things are not only taking up space, but they are also costing you opportunities—opportunities to sell them and get money to put into savings, pay off debt or buy something that is relevant to you now. When you sell something you don't want, need or use, you regain money and the space it was taking up. When you stockpile possessions, other people who are ready to use these possessions now are also losing opportunities to buy your things at a fraction of the retail cost. The fourth opportunity is for our environment. If we are selling and buying used, we decrease manufacturing and lessen our carbon footprint. And when we buy used and local, we slash the transportation impact on the environment.

The wedding dress that's usurping 25 percent of your closet space could sell at a consignment shop for eighty dollars; you would pocket about forty of those dollars. That makes for more closet space and extra money for you, a happy bride-to-be; plus it saves resources of producing a new dress. The best news is that you can get more for that dress on eBay, Craigslist, or niche sites such as woreitonce.com, preownedweddingdresses.com, or oncewed.com.

Seven Sites for Online Swapping

1. Freecycle.org is a grassroots and nonprofit movement of people who are giving and getting stuff for free in their own towns.
2. Craigslist.com has a section for free items.
3. TitleTrader.com lets you swap books, DVDs, or CDs with people around the world.
4. Swap.com brings people together to swap their stuff through the Swap website, mobile app, local events, homes, schools, and co-branded partnerships.
5. Rehashclothes.com is a fashionable way for you to trade your clothing, accessories, and books with others online.
6. Plasticjungle.com buys your unused gift cards and then sells them at a discount to others.
7. Swapright.com allows you to post offers to swap and barter services.

Got media? Sell your books, CDs, DVDs, and video games on Amazon.com or Half.com. These niche sites specifically target your prospective buyer; therefore, your items will sell faster and typically net a higher profit.

If you don't sell online or at a garage sale, take your clothes, accessories and, sometimes, toys to a consignment shop. Take your books, movies, and CDs to a media retailer that has a used section where you'll receive between 40 and 50 percent of the sale.

If you're ready to just be rid of the goods and don't feel like running around town, donate them. Go with either the most convenient location or a place that you personally want to support, such as a women's shelter, a children's hospital, or Coats for Kids.

If you have a neighborhood garage sale, you can call your local Goodwill and they will send a truck to pick up items that didn't sell. Remember, if you're donating items, take the time to list everything; you might as well get the full tax credit for it.

Making It Happen

As you evaluate every item in your home, you will witness a mass exodus of clutter from your home and car. Your car will look like you just drove off the dealer's lot with nothing more than sunglasses and a snowbrush in it. You'll be using rooms that you had previously abandoned. Treasures will surface, and you will enjoy them once more. You're going to be so organized that you'll no longer run to the store to buy something that you forgot you already had. You'll once again have a concept of your inventory.

When you have a manageable number of belongings, it will be easier to find a home for all of them. Creating a specific home for each of your belongings is the main secret to getting and staying organized. How can you find something or put something away if that object doesn't have a place to go? There should be only one place in your house where you put gifts that you are going to give someone (for me, it's in our suitcases), and the only thing in that place should be gifts. When your bungee cords are missing from their hook in the garage, you're going to ask who took them. No longer will you throw up your hands and decide it's easier to pick up a few at the store rather than dig through the abyss known as your garage. The abyss will no longer exist.

Two other secrets to staying organized are grouping similar items together and keeping items where you use them. Use these principles to find the perfect home for everything in your house.

I'll illustrate with an example of where to keep items you borrow from the library. (Keeping these items organized preserves the library as a source of free entertainment and not a source of anxiety because there's a ninety-eight dollar balance on your card.)

1. Designate a reusable tote for all library books and movies. I recommend a brightly colored, distinctive bag that serves as a visual reminder that you have library materials checked out. Hang this tote on a hook in your entryway. Everything must go into that bag when not in use. The only time items are out of the bag is when they're in use. Apply this principle to DVDs and books. It may take thirty seconds to return the book to the bag when you are done reading for the day, but that small investment will gain you five minutes when you don't have to hunt all over the house for the book.

2. Leave the library receipt in the bag and check the items against it before returning them, just in case something has grown legs. Five things on the list, five things in the bag. Check.

3. Plan a night out to the library. You don't have to check things out. You can spend a couple hours reading magazines or flipping through books without the responsibility of putting them on your account for seven days.

4. Have a specific library day. If you always go to the library on Wednesday, then it becomes part of your routine and you're not going to let items get wildly overdue.

5. Go electronic. E-PUBs and audio books are gaining momentum, and the public library is right there with the trend. The convenience of library e-content is twofold. First, you can browse material anytime you want from home. If the material is digitally checked out, you can be put on a waiting list, which will e-mail you when the item is available for download. After you download the material, the item will automatically expire from your computer without you having to pay attention to return dates. So, essentially there is never a late fee.

Note: You do not need to invest in an e-reader (e.g., Nook, Kindle, iPad) in order to enjoy the electronic content offered by the library. Programs such as Adobe Digital Editions and OverDrive Media Console are available for free download to your home computer. From there, you can listen or read directly off your computer from those host programs.

The Next Wave

Now that you have emotionally detached yourself from what is bringing you down, cramping your space, and limiting your freedom, you are more nimble and streamlined. You can appreciate something for a season and then let it go to someone else. You don't have to go to bed with it, just be glad you once had it. An item in your life is like a wave that you ride; it comes and goes. The good news is that another wave is coming. After you clear your slate, you will be open for more to come your way.

Slowing down naturally puts you in a mindset to be productive. As you start to see results, you'll build confidence and momentum. You're no lon-

Work From Home

My hope is that telecommuting positions become the norm in the decades to come. If you are interested in pursuing a telecommuting job, check out Flexjobs.com (paid membership required), Elance.com, and Guru.com.

ger the victim, but the champion. The positive energy that you radiate, now that your energy isn't being channeled into dead ends, will start to come back to you. You will attract what you seek because you'll have a clear understanding of what you want and need. You will be open to receive what is waiting for you. There will be no more Band-Aids for your feelings; you will be propelled forward toward goals rather than things.

When my husband and I made the decision for me to be a stay-at-home mom, we were able to make reductions in our life, like having one car. It was easy to sell our stuff because I was home to meet with potential buyers. There was no stress of getting kids on and off the school bus. We walked away from my salary, never anticipating that seven months later I would start working part-time out of our house. Over the next eighteen months, as my hours increased, my pay increased from one hundred dollars a week to a point where I was making 33 percent more than I was at my previous full-time job that was a thirty-five-minute commute each way.

If I had not walked away from my secure, full-time job, I would not have been open to accept the better position. When this transformation in my work life happened, I was reassured that reducing my lifestyle wasn't the road to being a recluse. I wasn't going to have less and less until I was void of modernization. I realized that this is when something better comes along. Something much better. Get rid of what's holding you back and open yourself up to what's next.

4: Find Your Pride

As a teenager, I was told a beautiful fable about a boy who caught a caterpillar. He put the caterpillar into a jar with plenty of leaves to eat. As time went on, the caterpillar formed its cocoon, and the boy patiently waited for the day when the caterpillar would emerge as a butterfly. The day finally arrived, and the boy could see the butterfly struggling to free itself from its cocoon. He watched the butterfly labor and strain against the resistance. He felt sorry for the butterfly, so he took his little fingers and opened the cocoon.

He expected the butterfly to open its wings and soar away. He thought he was that butterfly's hero. Instead, the butterfly couldn't even get out of the jar. Its wings were not strong enough to support it. The boy didn't realize that a butterfly builds up its strength through the challenge of opening its cocoon. The butterfly cannot survive on its own without that initial hardship. By relieving the butterfly of its temporary exertion, the boy ultimately caused the butterfly's demise.

I love this story. It gives me a grounded perspective when I see how far a do-it-yourself lifestyle can take people. Now, I'm not saying that you're an invalid if you cannot assemble your backyard swing set. But I am suggesting that your accomplishments will make you stronger. Becoming self-reliant opens a new appreciation for yourself and allows you to reach a level of joy that can be sustained. Yes, you can realize all this from learning and inserting your skills into daily life. Reduction Rebels have a do-it-yourself spirit that helps them learn new skills and discover new talents. This mindset reduces their dependency on commercial services while increasing the services they can offer to others (in the workplace, as a volunteer, or for friends and family). This chapter will help you develop this do-it-yourself attitude and walk you through basic projects you can do yourself.

Finding Time

It's easy to get sucked into sitting around watching reality TV, which populates hundreds of channels. What are these people on TV doing? They're not watching other people; they're living their lives. Make whatever judgments you want about them, but they are doing their thing. It's ironic that we would watch a typical day in their lives instead of having lives of our own.

If you have time to watch TV or mindlessly surf the Internet, you have time to engage in do-it-yourself projects and hobbies. We all need down time, but how often do you feel refreshed and invigorated after spending hours in front of a TV or computer monitor? It never happens, does it? Why? Because of inertia. It takes a lot more energy to get a stopped object in motion than to keep a moving object going. When you shut down in front of a screen, it seems like a momentous task to even take your drinking glass to the sink. Forget about working up the energy to cook dinner, engage in a hobby, or tackle a DIY project. And do you have anything to show for your time after watching all that TV? Nope, just lost time, which subconsciously adds to your stress by reducing the amount of productive time you have to meet your obligations.

It may seem stressful and time-consuming to do things yourself, but consider the rewards of using your time to take care of yourself. You'll save yourself money. You'll learn a new skill, and you'll actually burn stress because you used your time well and solved a problem or made an improvement, something to cross off your to-do list! And in doing all this, you'll find your pride. You'll give purpose to your free time and have interesting things to talk about with your friends. To heck with humility! Talk up your talents or your killer zucchini muffins made from scratch using your homegrown zucchini. Go ahead and be known for something!

The time is now to create a well-oiled, minimally complicated world for you to live in. Take control of the challenges that come your way so you can live easier, healthier, and wealthier. This is the path to finding new passions, sources of income, and quality time with those you love.

A Sense of Purpose

Have you ever met someone who gets way too much pleasure crossing items off his or her to-do list? These are the same people who post before-and-after pictures and invite strangers to see their latest creations. Motivational speaker Tamara Rowe calls this type of person a "producer." She

Exercise

Imagine reality TV cameras are filming your life (kind of like the movie, *EDtv* with Matthew McConaughey). What would you be doing? Who would be the co-stars? What channel would your show air on?

Now let's assume Mark Burnett is not going to walk through your door with a camera crew. More likely, the phone is going to ring. The person on the other end is going to ask what you're up to, and you're going to say… (ponder that one for as long as it takes to generate a respectable answer).

Exercise

I went to a bridal shower where the bride-to-be's sister made the cake. It had elaborate fondant bows and hearts. At the presentation of the cake, all the guests clapped for the sister's masterpiece. It would have been much easier to just buy a cake, but that would not have displayed her talents.

Where could your talents bring joy to others? Are you a whip at cleaning? Why not use your expertise as a housewarming gift for your niece who just moved into her first apartment? Those of you gifted in music could play for the elderly at your local community center or offer lessons through the classifieds section of your weekly paper.

Look around for groups or committees where you can network while strutting your stuff.

describes producers as competitive, creative, and quick decision makers. They are motivated by progress, opportunity, freedom to customize, flexibility, new choices, or simply a break from routine. Following through on projects and goals feels amazing. That shot in the arm that keeps them energized and free-spirited. They know what they can accomplish and how they can use their talents to sustain a positive attitude.

Opportunities for growth don't always have to come as problems. You can find them in new interests and activities. That's the beauty of talents; they can reach out into our friendships and communities.

Letting Go of Fears

Companies that sell services or products position their advertising toward consumers' fears. Fear is a compelling motivator in the retail area. What are people so afraid of? Well, one of the biggies is failure. We're afraid we're going to mess it up. "I'm not going to install wood flooring on my own because it might not look right," we tell ourselves. What's the worst that could happen? Certainly you're not going to wreck your entire stock of flooring. And you're definitely not going to dump the box out and start hammering. First, educate yourself, ask around for pointers, and get yourself best prepared. You'll want to conduct an Internet search for something like, "How to install wood flooring." Then go to a couple video sites and watch someone else do it. Next, do some searches on "tips for…" and "common problems when…". Then go for it. It's not going to kill you. And the best-case scenario is that you do an awesome job and you're jacked to tackle the next project.

Repair Instead of Replace

We all have possessions that mean something to us, whether they're sentimental, irreplaceable, or extremely useful. These things get preferential treatment, like protective storage or prominent display. We want these things to last. We want others to enjoy them. But how many things are on that list?

When something breaks or becomes outdated, we find ourselves saying, "Really, a new one only costs…". It's become so easy to replace our things—like everything is just a fad. Fad furniture, clothes, appliances, gadgets and décor. Here today, gone tomorrow.

Imagine if "Oh well" was not an acceptable answer when something was broken, worn, or scratched. What if buying another one was more challenging than a five-minute drive to a discount department store? For starters, there would be a revolution to demand better quality items. Then we'd all learn to revive what was starting to degenerate.

Because capitalism and mass-produced, foreign junk aren't going away anytime soon, we're going to find a middle ground in our reduction revolution. And moderation is good; it keeps you sane. You don't need to weave your own fabrics or hang onto dilapidated carpeting. But you will have opportunities to salvage your stuff by cleaning and repairing it. See the "DIY Home Décor Projects" section in this chapter and chapter five for step-by-step instructions on upcycling items around your home.

You probably already noticed things are not made like they used to be. You can easily tell by the look and feel if a product is cheap and will not go the distance. There's a reason a one-hundred-year-old bookcase is still in your living room while the ten-year-old particleboard entertainment center is out to the curb. There's not much you can do for something that was garbage to begin with.

Exercise

Do you have an old item in your home that you want to replace? Evaluate the "parts" on the item. Could you repair or change one of the parts and then continue to use the item? For example, if the armrests of your couch are tattered and stained, could you sew covers for them? Could you resurface or paint an end table to update it and make it more enjoyable? This may save a barrel of money and landfill waste and end up looking really cute.

Think about minor updates, where you can insert your talents rather than your credit card to get the results you need, not to mention the bragging rights.

When the engine seizes on your old, cast-iron garden tiller, you'll likely browse the stores for a new tiller. The new ones look shiny, but when you really investigate, don't you get that uneasy feeling that if you hit a tree root, that tiller is going to bite the dust? Because the new ones are made cheaper, you won't be able to replace your old tiller with a machine of equal quality. In cases like this, the more logical choice is to repair the broken item instead of replacing it. You keep the solid machine that will continue to last you many years instead of investing in something new that will likely need to be replaced in only a few years.

Clean to Be Green

Often, the easiest way to improve something is to simply clean it. Everything can be cleaned in one way or another. Cleaning provides satisfaction, exercise, and preservation. But so often, stains, scratches, spills and exposure to the elements can make us throw our hands up in defeat when we don't know the right product to use and the actions to take.

Here is a guide to cleaning solutions for common disasters so you can repair instead of replace.

1. *Paint on the Carpet.* We've all been there: The newspaper or drop cloth had a wrinkle in the exact, teensy spot of carpet where a

drip of paint dropped off our brush. We grab a wet sponge, but the paint is spreading. Don't have a panic attack, but do run. Get a wet washcloth, ring it out and fill it with ice cubes. Gather the corners of the washcloth so it looks like a small punching bag of ice. Twist the ice pouch into the paint area. The paint will transfer onto the washcloth. Even though this is like the Cat in the Hat where the stain now moves to the washcloth, it's better there than on your carpet.

2. *Blood on Fabric.* You want to console a bleeding child, but at the same time, you'd like to avoid blood stains on your clothes. Have no fear; peroxide is here. Apply peroxide to a cloth and wipe the blood from your stained clothing, furniture, carpet, whatever.

3. *Oil on Fabric.* If peanut butter, salad dressing, or fried food drips onto your clothes, do you have a conniption? You frantically pre-treat, scrub and wash, but know deep down that when it comes out of the dryer, you will find a grease spot on the garment. A three-dollar bottle of Lestoil will save you time, energy, and stress. The trick to success is timing. Apply the Lestoil a few minutes before washing. It cannot go on at the last minute, and it can't sit on the stain for hours. Three to five minutes will do the job right.

4. *Tarnished Metals.* Whether it's a teapot, silverware, or drawer handles, over time these metal household items are going to discolor and tarnish. Here's how to tackle the tarnish:

Before

After

- *Silver:* Place in a container lined with aluminum foil so all the silver is in contact with the foil. Fill with water and shake baking soda and salt evenly over the silver. Let it sit for several hours.
- *Brass:* Make a paste of lemon juice and baking soda. Let it fizz and then settle. Apply with a cloth or your fingers. No worries, it's all natural!
- *Unlacquered Copper:* Apply tomato paste with a spatula and let it sit for one to two hours. This will remove the light tarnish, which may be all you need. If there are tough spots, scrub with half a lemon that's been dipped in salt. If this doesn't completely do the trick, buy Brasso. Sometimes, years of neglect need a bit of harsh chemicals, but try the natural route first.

5. *Rusted Chrome:* Squirt WD-40 on the chrome piece. Next, crumple up a ball of foil and work it back and forth in a linear motion (circular motion is said to show minor scratching). Buff to a shiny finish using an old T-shirt.

Who knew regular household items could transform rusty, pitted chrome back to its original luster? When my son and I came across a 1950s chrome breadbox in a garbage pile, I insisted that we leave it there. I didn't think there was any hope for restoration. My son insisted that it must go home with us. He won.

After doing the research and finding that everything I needed to fix it was already in my house, it was a slam-dunk restoration. Our efforts were met with almost instant satisfaction (especially the buffing part) and utter excitement to welcome its classic, functional design into our kitchen. We even went so far as to send a picture and thank-you note to the people who threw it out. We were that proud!

Take Back Your Tasks

Many personal and domestic tasks can be accomplished by regular people who have the patience to learn, try, and try again. The last time my boys went to the barber, it cost thirty dollars for two haircuts. That was several years ago. Since then, my family has invested in an electric hair trimmer. My husband and I watched a handful of videos on YouTube before embark-

Exercise

What do you have around the house that could use a shine? Take into account that you likely have the supplies needed to bring the sparkle back to your brass picture frames or copper bookends. Go for it. It will brighten your rooms and leave a refreshing, lemon-fresh scent.

What have you cleaned lately that gave you serenity? Was it a sparkling shower or crumb-free counters? Now think about something you've cleaned that actually cancelled a trip to the store to make a replacement purchase. Did you rub toothpaste on the *Lion King* DVD so your child's favorite movie could live on? Or have you power-washed the algae off your patio instead of building a deck? Big or small, cleaning versus replacing can provide quicker satisfaction and eco-friendly solutions.

ing on the task in our backyard. I'll admit, it was a little nerve-racking at first. It probably took an hour to cut each child's hair, but we remained patient. Our trimmers have easily paid for themselves many times over. Now we could have borrowed someone's trimmers to see if this was going to work for us, but by making the investment up front, we gave ourselves no choice but success. With no initial investment, we could have easily gotten frustrated and given up after the first try. This was a safe and fairly simple task to take on—we're talking about haircuts, not heart surgery.

This same attitude can be applied to everything from waxing your eyebrows to replacing drywall. The more we learn to do things for ourselves, the more money we save, the better our homes look, and the more independent we become. I don't want to have to take my pants to a tailor when I need a hem shortened. I don't want to book a caterer every time I host a party at my house. And I definitely don't want to call a plumber every time a foreign object accidentally gets flushed down the toilet. No way.

This is a very important mind-set in the reduction movement. It's important because it helps form the good habits of creating our own things and being handy.

Here are some tasks you can take back for yourself:

Beauty/Grooming:

basic men's haircuts

trimming bangs

manicure/pedicure

shaping your eyebrows

sugar waxing

Lawn/Garden:

mow your lawn

shovel your driveway

rake your leaves

grow your own herbs and
vegetables

paint your house

roof your house

clean your gutters

put up your patio canopy

arrange and plant perennials

till your garden

spread grass fertilizer

lawn edging

Domestic:

cook at home instead of dining
at a restaurant

rent or purchase a carpet
cleaner

rearrange furniture

hang window treatments

hem pants

mend clothing

Trouble-Shoot Before You Replace

I confess, in the past I've bought into the mind-set that it's easier to replace than repair. When my German-built showerhead started acting a little fussy, I went to the local big-box store and bought a shiny, new showerhead made in China.

I removed my old showerhead and realized it was full of water deposits. I cleaned out the deposits, and the old showerhead was as good as new. The replacement went back to the store, and I learned an important lesson.

Become a Pro

Take a gander at what efforts you delegate to others (usually for payment). Do you hire someone to put up holiday decorations? Do you go to a salon to get your hair dyed? Does a professional (or teenager) detail your car?

The next time you hire a professional, pay attention to the tools they are using. Is it equipment that you already have (like a sponge and a vacuum) or something that would be worth the investment (a jigsaw)? Run the numbers. You might save more money if you do it yourself.

Consider the risks. As long as there's no asbestos or a tight spring that could rip your fingers off, it might be a no-brainer to try doing something yourself instead of hiring someone else to do it for you.

Home Maintenance:

- paint and/or wallpaper rooms
- set up technology
- install appliances (like a dishwasher)
- repair or replace roof shingles
- drain the hot water tank to remove sediment (recommended annually)
- change water purification filters/furnace filters

Some people believe that education is the single greatest way to get ahead in this world; others would argue experience is more important. I say it's both. We must always be reaching to learn new principles and skills, but it isn't until we put them into practice that the lesson is complete.

Lucky for us, now more than ever, information is ever-present in our lives. We just need to be proactive in seeking and utilizing that information. Are the hours you spend surfing the web used to look at photos from other people's lives, or are they spent learning how to do something for yourself?

Handy Around the House

If your quest is to become more self-sufficient, there are some basic home maintenance tasks you can handle on your own. I'm far from a home-improvement expert or professional handyman, but I have tackled some recurring tasks as a homeowner that saved me time, trouble, and money. In some way, the skills I've outlined have empowered me, improved my quality of life, or provided peace of mind. This may mean using up a lot of your time at first, but remember, you are learning a new skill. The next time will be a breeze. If there's two feet of water in your basement, this is not the time to learn a new skill. When you have the time (because you've already reduced the needless maintenance and obligations in your life), conquer the challenge.

Reduction Rebel Basic Tool Set

Tools assist your skills. The reduction process requires some essential tools to make your life easier and more self-sufficient. A computer with a high-speed Internet connection and a printer is always helpful. You can find tutorials and trouble-shooting advice for any project you tackle. Below is a recommended list of helpful tools you'll want to start collecting for your own Reduction Rebel toolkit. This is not a list of mandatory items that you need to run out and buy, but if you can get your hands on something, seize the opportunity.

hammer	toilet plunger
screwdrivers (straight and Philips head)	level
	drill
needle-nose pliers	wood filler
adjustable wrenches	wood glue
drain plunger	sandpaper

Five Resources for Helpful How-tos

vimeo.com
www.instructables.com
www.ehow.com
www.wikihow.com
makezine.com

Did You Know

Did you know three Alka-Seltzer tablets and a cup of white vinegar, followed minutes later by hot water, has been known to unclog a drain? If you don't have Alka-Seltzer, use a ¼ cup of baking soda.

The DIY Plumbing Toolbox

Some plumbing problems require a professional, but you can fix many common, minor problems, such as drips, clogs, and items flushed down a toilet or dropped down a drain, yourself using inexpensive tools and a little online searching. Here's what you need:

A *closet auger:* This looks like a rod in the shape of a hockey stick with a handle that cranks in a motion like a butter churn. This nonelectric device will put your toilet troubles to rest by clearing major blockages and retrieving improperly flushed debris. When the toilet paper roll holder was accidentally flushed down the toilet at my house, a closet auger saved the day, and we were able to get the holder out without calling a plumber or taking apart pipes.

Teflon tape: It fills any gaps between pipe threading to ensure that you get a watertight seal on threaded pipe joints. This is what you'll use to put an end to your dripping showerhead or faucet. Keep in mind there is a science to how this tape is applied, so explore instructions online.

Plumber's putty: This seals areas not subjected to water pressure, like a drain.

Pipe wrench: It's the iconic wrench with the adjustable toothed grip used to clench down on rounded objects, like pipes, and a nut that's been stripped. This is just one of those catchall toolbox staples.

DIY Home Décor Projects

Reducing consumption and waste is a big part of being a Reduction Rebel. How often do we get rid of a piece of furniture because it becomes damaged or we want to update the style in our home? A few basic craft supplies and a little creativity can repair or update any piece of furniture—even those you see sitting on the curb waiting for the garbage truck.

The following four projects will help you bring new style to your home. Each project has a supply list with it, but you will want a few general supplies for your toolbox. Again, this is not an exhaustive list, and you don't need to run out and buy everything right away. These are helpful tools to collect as you have the means to purchase them.

Toolbox for Upcycling and Craft Projects

fabric tacks, large and small	decorative paper
decorative duct tape	tracing light box
Mod Podge	double-sided tape
sewing machine	felt-tip permanent markers
fabric, thread, needles, pins	T-square
measuring tape	stencils
fabric pencil	foam paper
sharp scissors	stickers, labeling supplies
cutting mat	acrylic paints and brushes
craft knife	hot glue gun

PROJECT 1:

Upholstering a Tabletop or Seat

Upholstering a piece of furniture is a great way to extend its life, which saves you money. In my home, I have found four instances where covering a tabletop or seat was a necessary solution:

1. *Child safety:* Our coffee table had, what I considered, sharp corners, and I was afraid my wobbly toddlers might fall into them. So I thought a cushioned fabric top would rectify the situation in a very tasteful manner. You can buy cushioned corner protectors at baby supply stores, but they're unattractive and only useful for those few years that kids are getting their balance. The Reduction Rebel is in it for the long haul. When given the choice of temporary fix or aesthetic solution, we go for the latter. We strive for quality and obsolescence.

2. *Hiding damage or a flaw:* Did your son or daughter chip the heck out of your coffee table with the TV remote, Bamm-Bamm Rubble style? Are you thinking of passing over an estate sale chair that has paint drips on the seat? Is there a crack down the center? All of these imperfections can be solved with some fabric and quilt batting.

3. *Updating décor:* Mauve flowers are out. Blue seersucker doesn't work in the art deco dining room. Tattered or stained fabric needs a face-lift. Recovering the surface is much more practical than replacing the piece altogether, or hiring someone else to do it for you. The local fabric store has a stellar selection of home décor fabrics—and don't forget to check the remnant bins for discount fabrics. Think of the possibilities!

4. *Making the piece more functional or appealing:* Sometimes we look at a lackluster piece of furniture and realize all it needs is some softening. Yes, furniture can be as unapproachable as some people. Feel it out. Is it cold, stiff, drab, or about to put a splinter in your rear? Time for a comfy upgrade.

MATERIALS

Fabric of choice (home décor fabrics; canvas and pleather are recommended)

Quilt batting (enough for a single cut; pieces won't give a smooth enough finish)

Scissors

Measuring tape

Fabric pencil

Iron

Hammer covered with a sock or soft fabric

Small fabric tacks

Upholstery tacks; screwdriver; needle-nose pliers (optional)

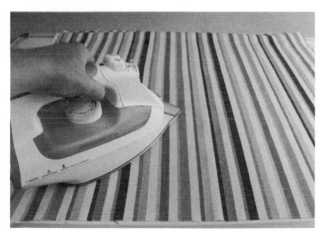

1. If this is a re-cover job, unscrew the seat cushion from the chair and pull out the existing tacks.

2. Cut the batting and fabric a few inches longer than the size of the tabletop or seat surface you're covering. The fabric should extend an inch longer than the batting to allow for a fabric hem, which will keep the batting from sticking out past the fabric on the underneath edges.

3. Fire up your iron and run it over the fabric to make sure it's smooth and all the creases are out. While you have the iron out, iron a ½" (13mm) fold along the fabric perimeter. This is essentially a hem so that, over time, rogue strings don't hang down from the chair bottom.

4. On a hard surface, place the fabric print-side down. Place the batting, centered, on the fabric. Then place the tabletop or wood piece in the center of the batting.

5. Press down on the center of the piece you are covering so the fabric can be pulled tight around to the underside. Another person or a heavy object can help you press down the piece. (In the picture you'll see that I've used a marble brick as a weight.) If this is a one-person job, use your foot or knee to apply the necessary pressure and keep your hands free. After the fabric and batting are snug around the wood, begin hammering in fabric tacks. Be sure the fabric is folded over neatly. It may seem like this is a dexterous task, but after you poke the little tacks into the fabric, they'll stand up well enough that you can hammer without trying to hold them up.

6. (Optional) If you find the fabric is a bit loose when you flip over your finished piece, you can always add upholstery tacks to tighten it up. The bigger the surface, the more likely the fabric will be loose. So be sure to gauge how many tacks will look appropriate. In a long, narrow coffee table, three might do the trick. In a chair, one in the center is good. Before you whack the tack, be sure to cover the hammer with a sock or soft fabric. This will buffer the hammer and keep it from damaging the tack.

Here is a before-and-after look at the upholstered chair seat project, and a friendly reminder to always take before-and-after photos of your work. It really enhances the conversation piece.

Before

After

83

PROJECT 2:
Putting Up a Shelf

Shelving is the easiest option for clutter control, vertical storage, and inexpensive decorating. Shelves make collections, knickknacks, and keepsakes look and feel important and organized. After we first bought our home, my husband and I had a motto: another weekend, another shelf. We put up shelves for our cookbooks. We installed one under the bathroom mirror to hold our soap dish and some guest hand towels. We even put a shelf in our stairway simply to add visual interest. We got our stuff off the floor, flat surfaces, and workspaces, and used it to liven up our bare walls.

It may seem daunting to put a hole in a freshly painted wall, but trust me—you'll be better for having done it.

Here's how you go about putting up a shelf with decorative brackets. This kind of shelf has maximum flexibility because you buy the brackets separate from the shelf so you have control over the shelf length and style.

MATERIALS

Shelf	Screwdriver
Metal brackets	Hammer (if using screw anchors)
Stud finder or screw anchors	Level
Drill	Pencil

1. Start by measuring the length of your shelf and marking its position properly within your space.

2. If you plan to drill into the studs (wooden supports behind drywall), you will need a stud finder so you know where to line up your bracket. If you're not going into the studs, be sure to have screw anchors. For my demo, I'm using anchors.

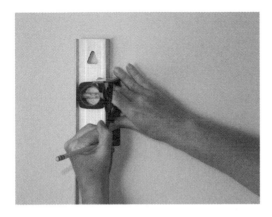

3. Hold a level in a vertical position up against your bracket and mark the screw holes with a pencil.

4. Drill into the penciled circle and then hammer the screw anchors into the drill hole. As you can see in the image with the drill, the screw anchor has been hammered into the top hole.

5. Screw the bracket into the screw anchors in the wall.

6. Rest your shelf on the single attached bracket without screwing it in place. Rest your level on the shelf until it is even and then hold the second bracket in position. Mark the bracket holes in pencil.

7. Repeat the drilling, anchor insertion, and screwing process for the second bracket. Place the shelf on the brackets. From below, screw the shelf into the brackets.

Spray-Painting Furniture

Put down your brushes and experience the quick-drying, multipurpose painting method with very little cleanup: spray-painting. Spray-paint works on everything from metal to plastic to wood. There's even fabric spray-paint, which is seriously cool. Spray-paint leaves a smooth finish, which is especially important if you're painting something for outdoor use. The brushstrokes of traditional paint leave small grooves that can hold moisture that will reduce the life of outdoor furniture.

Are there some drawbacks to consider? Yes. For example, if you have numerous areas that need to be masked off, masking the areas will consume a lot of tape and time. If that's the case, you may want to opt for the control of hand painting. Also, if you have a large project, it may be cost prohibitive as those three-to-four-dollar cans of spray-paint can empty faster than you think.

Picking the Paint

If you're freshening up a utilitarian piece, try to keep colors close to the originals. This keeps recoats to minimum. But if the piece is decorative, you can get as crazy with the colors as you want. There's been some whining about limited color selection in the spray-paint aisle. True, you probably aren't going to get a spot-on match to your drapes because there's no customized mixing like in traditional paint. But check out the selection; it's beyond hunter green, barn red, and antique white. Today, spray-paint comes in bright bolds, classics, myriad neutrals, and even unique finishes. I just recommend that you don't waste your money on one-dollar cans because these will end up costing you time and money in the long run.

The one thing about spray-painting is that it's a fair weather project. I like to wait until I have decent weather so I can do the job outside, or at least with my basement well ventilated. Also, don't think it's overkill to wear protective goggles and a mask.

MATERIALS

Spray primer (optional)

Spray-paint

Fine sandpaper

Painter's tape (optional to mask areas)

Goggles

Mask

Prepping the Project

1. To start, make sure your surface area is clean and rough areas are sanded down. Be sure to take off any knobs or handles.

2. Use spray primer if you're working with something that's never been painted or in high contrast to the color you're about to apply. The primer has a tendency to leave a slight texture. Should that be the case, give it a once-over with your fine sandpaper.

3. When applying the paint, the best technique is to use broad, circular strokes (wax on, wax off) and let up on the trigger from time to time.

Before

After

You're not killing a bug; you're gracefully applying color. It's better to go back for a second coat than to spray the heck out of it and get drip marks. Likely, you will need an extra coat, so give the paint a chance to dry before hitting the item again.

Finishing Touches

After your piece is consistently painted, you may want to consider

- adding a stencil
- distressing by using fine to medium sandpaper. Rub off the new paint on the edges to expose the previous paint color or natural wood underneath.
- applying a polycrylic or polyurethane sealer to create a polished look. This also protects your piece and makes it easier to clean.

How to Make Your Own Stencils

You can buy a wide selection of furniture stencils at craft stores, but if you're looking for something custom, you'll have to make it. This isn't a biggie, though.

1. Find a clean, flat plastic lid such as those used for sour cream, cottage cheese, or margarine. If the lid has a raised ring around the outer edge, cut it off so it lays completely flat. This will be your stencil.
2. Draw your custom image onto the plastic piece.
3. Use a craft knife to cut out where you want the paint to fill in on your image.
4. Attach the stencil to the furniture with painter's tape to keep it in place while you are painting. Apply stencil adhesive around the opening of the stencil design to keep the paint from flowing underneath so you get a sharp edge.

How to Make Simple Curtains

Sewing curtains, pillowcases, and tea towels is easy and an affordable way to decorate your home. The gateway to sewing is simply threading the sewing machine. Consult your machine's manual for instruction on how to thread it. If you don't have a manual, do an online search; you should be able to find the manual (or at least one for a similar model) or order one from the manufacturer. After your thread and bobbin are in place, you're ready to rock.

If you're new to sewing, get some scrap fabric and practice sewing a straight line. Practice makes you familiar and comfortable with your sewing machine and takes the pressure off of ruining good fabric.

When starting out, I say start square. Making rod-pocket curtains is a fast, easy way to give a room a face-lift, and it's a great beginner's project. With so many fabrics to choose from, you can achieve a custom look on a conservative budget.

MATERIALS

Sewing machine

Fabric (see below for size and material)

Thread that matches your fabric

Tape measure

Sharp scissors

Iron

Straight pins

Drape weights (iron fishing lure weights or nickels)

Selecting and Measuring Your Fabric

Choose nice fabric. Curtains are not only on prominent display in your home, but they also serve two important functions: privacy and sun blockage. Thin, poorly made fabric will not be effective. Plus, you don't want to spend time and money on something you won't be happy with in the end. So be sure to select fabric that is both pretty and substantial. Measure the window to determine how much fabric you'll need.

To determine the width of your two curtain panels, measure the width of your window frame, add 4" (10cm) and divide by 2.

To determine the length, measure the length from curtain rod to the bottom of the window frame. Add 7" (18cm).

1. Cut your fabric to the size you calculated following the instructions. Iron the fabric so it is smooth and wrinkle-free.

2. Double fold the side hems. Fold the sides of your curtain panels ½" (13mm) and then another ½" (13mm) so that the cut edge is tucked in. Iron down the hem and then pin it in place. Sew.

3. Make the top casing. Along the top of the curtain, fold the top of the fabric over ½" (13mm), iron, and then fold it down 3" (76mm) and iron. Pin the hem in place. Measure 1½" (38mm) from the top fold. Run pins through the fabric to mark this seam. The curtain rod will slide in between these two seams, allowing for the extra 1½" (38mm) top fold to ruffle above the curtain rod.

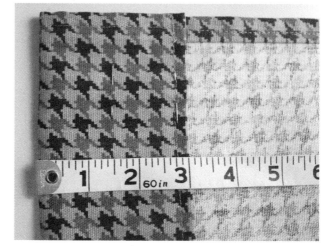

4. Weight the bottom hem. Fold the bottom over ½" (13mm), iron, and then fold it another 1" (25mm), iron, pin, and sew. This will leave enough room to insert drape weights. You don't need to buy special weights. You can raid the fishing tackle box for iron lures or just use nickels. Position the weights in the inside corners of the bottom hem. Sew the hem on either side of the weights to keep them contained.

Helpful Sewing Resources

1. www.sewweekly.com
2. sewing.patternreview.com
3. shwinandshwin.blogspot.com
4. *Through the Needle* (free online magazine) www.berninausa.com/content-n852-sUS.html
5. *A Guide to Fashion Sewing* by Connie Amaden-Crawford
6. *Reader's Digest Complete Guide to Sewing*
7. *Simplicity's Simply the Best Sewing Book*

DIY Photography

I love photography, so I decided to invest in a quality camera to capture pictures of my children whenever I want instead of relying on a professional studio to create "special memories." Whether you take your kids to a professional photographer or snap a candid at the playground, the result is the same—you have captured their image.

Going to a professional studio requires making an appointment and then praying that mealtime, the nap schedule, and bowel movements are all perfectly aligned so you can get the precious shot in that twenty-minute window. You sweat through squeaky toys and flashes, holding a forced smile and a steady, bright-eyed gaze. When the most acceptable shot is agreed upon, you're then put through the sales ringer on spending more than the $7.99 promotion. The whole process is an uphill battle.

Now, enter you and your camera. You have the flexibility to take the picture when the moment is right, when it's natural. With your own camera, you get to have great photos of what you want on your time, in your space and under your control. A great camera doesn't just save you the cost of school pictures, holiday cards, and special-occasion portraits; it's something that you could use almost every day in a reduction lifestyle. You can take fabulous pictures of the items you're selling on Internet sites, such as Craigslist and eBay. You can get detailed close-ups of any imperfections or unique markings so buyers know exactly what they're getting, reducing the chance for time-consuming returns. And hey, why not use your camera for eye candy on your blog? Or it might be just what you need to start your own online enterprise.

A quality camera purchase is an investment that is practical and useful, and provides cost and time savings. This isn't a bike that's going to get you up an incline more easily; it's a tool. Be sure to make that distinction. Tools assist our skills; they're not meant to do the work for us. What other tools have you invested in that brought improvement and empowerment?

Cooking From Scratch

There are several theories on where the cooking term "from scratch" came from. Some say it originated in the nineteenth-century athletic scene of boxing and cricket, indicating the starting point scratched into the ground.

Five Tips for Better Photos

1. *Read your camera's manual.* Seriously, sit down on a quiet day and read about all the functions. Then try them out. See what you like in relation to different subject matter.
2. *Test your light.* I prefer to take my photos outside. I find it's easier to work with the natural light. If going outside is not possible or convenient, I highly recommend building a light box for taking small close-up or product shots. Check out the article http://digital-photography-school.com/how-to-make-a-inexpensive-light-tent.
3. *Clear out the background.* Your subject matter gets compromised when there is clutter in the background. Move to an open space or opt for an aerial shot where the background is more limited and controlled.
4. *Move in close.* Whether it's faces or products, don't be afraid to get right in there. While you're up close, play with eye contact. Have the subject interacting with something else.
5. *Go for action.* It's one thing to capture smiles; it's another thing to capture personality. Try action shots over poses. Have some fun with it. After all, why act like you're stuck in a studio with a fake background when you have the freedom to be yourself?

Another sports-related origin is a golfer without a handicap. All I know is that it generally means starting without an advantage and working with basics: unaltered, singular ingredients coming together to create a recipe. It's the opposite of using boxed or prepackaged food. Cooking from scratch is part of the Reduction Rebel's lifestyle because it reduces

- the amount of preservatives and chemicals you eat
- the amount of food packaging you throw away
- the amount of money you spend on groceries (compare price per serving and you'll find premade meals and convenience foods are way more expensive than made-from-scratch meals)
- the distance your food traveled to reach you (especially if you grow your own food or shop at farmers markets)

Exercise

Think about boxed or processed items that you may rely on to save time. Could these things be made in a healthier fashion on the weekend and then frozen for use throughout the week? How about foods like uncrusted PB&J sandwiches or breaded chicken pieces? Who says you can't do the prep work using organic and whole wheat ingredients and then freeze them? Take it a step further. When you're making a homemade potpie, why not make two and freeze one? While you have all the ingredients, measuring tools, and cookware out, why not do a little extra work for double the outcome? It can be your "free cooking pass" waiting in the freezer for a night when you need some extra R&R.

My especially green sister (think cloth diapers) spent the day before her son's birthday making three cakes from scratch. Then I had a thought. I should make a cake from scratch; how hard could it be? Nothing like a little sibling rivalry to reunite me with my mixing bowls. So I cracked open good ol' Betty Crocker and had a look-see: flour, sugar, butter, (check), milk, baking powder, salt, (yep, got it) vanilla, and eggs (yeah, covered there).

So what I'm saying is, I, and most likely you, pretty much could whip up an all-natural cake "from scratch" any day of the week. There was no search for vanilla beans or crème fraîche, or figuring out yeast packets. See, scratch just sounds difficult. Try it. It'll look good on you.

Of course, it will be easier to cook if you have the equipment you need. You probably have all of these already:

pots and pans	colander/strainer
baking sheets	mixing bowls
bakeware	wooden spoons
quality knife set	spatulas
cutting board	electric hand mixer
measuring cups and spoons	

Scratch Solutions

When my son started kindergarten, I was able to cut our morning routine down to nine minutes. This was nothing short of a miracle in motion. We rose at 8:19, and he boarded the bus at 8:28 with a once-frozen, toasted waffle in hand. Yes, our streamlined hustle hinged on the box of six frozen waffles we bought each week at three dollars a box. That sounds pretty cheap until one fateful weekend we went to a farmers market and came home with a quart of buttermilk. There was nowhere for the buttermilk to go except into pancakes—the best pancakes I've ever eaten.

Now, making pancakes from scratch takes significantly longer than nine minutes, but who says I have to make pancakes every morning? My son was already eating pre-frozen waffles I brought home from the store. Why couldn't I make a big batch of pancakes on the weekend and freeze them for use during the week? We still save time, and now we are saving money and eating higher-quality food instead of over-processed food stripped of most of its nutritional value.

Buttermilk Pancakes

- 2 cups buttermilk
- 1 peeled, cored and pummeled apple
- 2 eggs, beaten
- 2 tablespoons granulated sugar
- 1 cup wheat flour
- 1 cup white, all purpose flour
- 2 teaspoons Baking Powder
- 1 teaspoon Baking Soda

In a bowl, combine buttermilk, apple, eggs and sugar. Mix well. In a separate bowl, combine the flours, baking powder, and baking soda. Mix well, then add dry ingredients to the wet ingredients.

Lube up your nonstick electric griddle and start pouring out some circles of heaven! Flip the pancakes when you see bubbles in the batter.

Freshen It Up

When you're done thinking about the boxed food in your freezer, shift your attention to your jarred food situation, things like pickles, preserves, and salsa. We buy them in jars for their long shelf lives. This means that once-fresh produce can be hanging around on your shelves for up to a year before you eat it. I do understand the appeal. It can be overwhelming to try to consume two cups of salsa in a couple of days. You may feel pressure to beat the expiration date or grow bored with the redundancy of including fresh apricot jam in every meal for two weeks.

But here's the real question: have you ever eaten these delicacies fresh—as in, never-been-cooked for the canning process? My neighbor brought over a twist-sealed jar of freezer jam one summer. She told me I had two weeks to eat it or I could freeze it for up to a year. The strawberries had been crushed and mixed with sugar, lemon juice, and pectin, but not cooked at all. I practically drank this jam with a straw. It was so delicious. My kids were dunking crackers in it. We were downright slobs about it. That's because we had never tasted jam that fresh. It was worth the time limit!

Same goes for raw salsa. You cannot get enough of the off-the-vine taste. Think of it like eating a salad. People eat salads the size of clam buckets. So why wouldn't you down six ounces of fresh salsa in a sitting?

In an attempt to creatively use an avocado that was becoming over-ripe, I gave birth to an original Avocado Clementine Salsa that is to die for. I had delusions that I would share the dish with my husband, but that did not happen. I selfishly scarfed down the whole thing.

This is what can happen when you taste pure, unaltered food. Our bodies crave the dense nutrients and the simplicity. There are benefits found in our energy level, outward appearance, and pocketbook. Now I'm not asking that you step back into the 1800s to kill your meat and cook it all day. There is a very good reason we're no longer living like the pioneers. I'm just advocating the use of quality, natural ingredients for a healthier lifestyle. Don't be shy about experimenting. I'm sure you've done it before.

The Revival of Customization

Here's an interesting observation. One hundred and fifty years ago, people routinely made their own soap, bread, and even homes out of necessity.

Avocado Clementine Salsa

1 tablespoon lemon juice

1 tablespoon honey

½ teaspoon salt

Dash of cayenne pepper

2 tablespoons minced red onion

1 Clementine (peeled and cut-up, contain the juices)

½ of a small bell pepper, chopped

1 ripe avocado

Mix and mash the ingredients together. Serve immediately. Refrigerate the leftovers.

This recipe can easily be doubled or tripled.

Helpful tip: If, by chance, there are leftovers, add your avocado pit back into the salsa. This will help prevent the avocado from browning. Just remember to remove it before serving again.

Fifteen years ago, people made their own ice cubes. This is a foreign concept to my kids because, today, if you want ice, you press a button on your refrigerator door. What else is going to be a foreign concept? Opening our own car doors? Washing our own hair? I'm not sure, but I did notice that kids today want to decorate their own sneakers, and some adults like to mix their own tea blends. This modern, do-it-yourself concept goes by a fancier name—customizing. Who knew that 150 years later we would be making our own soap for the joy of it so we can include pleasures like orange peels and poppy seeds? We don't have to let entitlement, technology, and convenience weaken us. We can use these things when and where it makes sense, and when we want something they can't give us, we can create it ourselves. The tasks we take back and the things we repair are ours to make unique. If someone's doing it for you, the result will be the same as the next guy's. When it's in your hands, it's exclusive to your taste and individuality. It's your creative outlet, motivation, and source of pride. Own it.

5: Lessons in Upcycling

Upcycling is an awesome way to give old, unwanted objects new life, either as better incarnations of their original selves or as raw materials that can be rebuilt in a different way to serve a new function. You have the power to help garbage graduate to one-of-a-kind greatness. This process goes beyond a project; it's an evolution of creativity brought on by need and emotions. Have you ever looked at an old, unwanted object and felt sorry for it? I'll look at an old rocking chair and think it doesn't deserve to be an eyesore; it should be remade into something that is loved. Okay, maybe that's just me. But surely you've looked at something no longer used in your home and wished there were a way to get more use out of it. Upcycling let's you do just that. You don't need to throw out what you have to make room for what you need. You can turn what you have into what you need.

Reducing waste and making useful, interesting things that revive your home are within your control. I like to call this "new it yourself." Convert an old T-shirt into a pillow and shazam! It's new to you. Or how about transforming two plates and a candle holder into a two-tiered display for your cupcakes? Who can tell that your neighbor threw out the plates and candle holder after her garage sale? Certainly not the folks adoring your cupcakes. Yes, I did say the neighbor threw them out, meaning they were in her garbage on the curb. There's no better place to find old, unwanted items, ripe for an upcycling pick, than on the curb the night before garbage day. But if the idea of garbage-picking is not for you, I'm sure you'll have no trouble finding old items in your home that deserve a new life. It's a great way to get rid of clutter and meet a need within your home.

This chapter walks you through the upcycling process. You'll learn what resources and materials you'll need for upcycling and where to find them. I will be your creative mentor on repurposing and fixing up broken and damaged items, and transforming easy-to-find furniture pieces into practical household commodities and unique conversation pieces. Now get out the hand salve because you may get some blisters!

Solutions for Your Home

Have you ever MacGyvered a dartboard into a lazy Susan? Or converted a beaker into a makeshift vase? What about using PVC pipes as shoe compartments in a hall closet, or refurbishing a battered desk with funky colors in a single weekend? When you let your creativity take over, the possibilities are endless. And as you elevate the beauty and purpose of the things around you, you'll find so much satisfaction in your upcycled projects.

In the context of this book, we're looking for ideas for our homes. We want to upcycle things that will help us make our homes our happiness headquarters. Identify problems you need to solve in your home. Examples could be: *I need to furnish every room in my downstairs. My mother-in-law is coming, and she needs a first-floor bedroom. My backyard has no privacy. It's time for the spare bedroom to become a crafting room.* After you've identified the problem, you can have fun and get creative with the solution.

When looking for a solution, start by brainstorming; it's a great way to jump-start your creativity. Share your problem with family and friends, and

Exercise

List five things you need or want for your home.

Now list five things you want to get rid of in your home. Give this list some thought. Walk around and see what is and isn't working. Identify items you haven't used in years or have never really liked.

When both lists are complete, brainstorm ways to upcycle the items you no longer want into the items you do want or need.

ask for their ideas. Try e-mailing a survey to your friends or posting your query on social media sites like Twitter or Yahoo! Answers. Search Google Images, Flickr or Pinterest for visual inspiration. Keep an open mind and check criticism and immediate analysis at the door.

Everyday Upcycling

I think of my recycling bin as garbage purgatory. My glass, plastic, and paper sit in the bin for up to a week before the items either leave in the waste management truck or are welcomed back into my home. I can't save every cardboard toilet paper roll or spinach container for when a need arises—the clutter is counterproductive and unnecessary (I know more is coming). So I put the items in the bin for disposal, but if I find I need something, I am committed to running there first. Think about where you keep your recycling bin. Does anything in it ever get a second chance?

Review your recycling bin for reusable items. Without going out of your way or becoming obsessive, try to incorporate your recyclables back into use. Think of your tossed-out cardboard and cream cheese containers when you're doing your projects. I've provided some practical reuse suggestions for things frequently found in a recycle bin. Use paint, decorative paper and Mod Podge to beautify and elevate these objects, and you'll enjoy them even more.

Egg Carton: Hang it up to make a bulletin board or calendar. It's easy to pin reminders and permission slips to them. Or use them to separate shared snacks; everyone gets his or her own section full of M&Ms. Better yet, position an opened carton in the bottom of your kitchen garbage can to catch any leaks from the liner.

Soup Can: Container for keys, pencils; desktop or drawer organizers.

Yogurt Cup: Container for starter plants; homemade Popsicle cups.

Adhesive Bandage Box: Holder for ointment tubes in your bathroom cabinet—they fit perfectly on those narrow shelves and keep those tubes organized.

Paper Towel Roll: Vacuum attachment that bends to fit in tight places like under and between major appliances.

Spaghetti Sauce Jar: Take hot food on the go with a leak-proof lid and glass that's microwave safe.

Newspaper: Soak newspaper and lay it in your flower beds and garden to prevent weeds. Cover with soil.

Milk Jug: A watering can—heat a pin to melt holes in the cap. Or fill with water or gravel to make exercise weights. As you get stronger, you can increase the weight.

Baby Wipes Container: Fill with supplies for a car emergency kit. The sturdy plastic and snap lid make this a perfect travel container, no matter the contents.

Laundry Detergent Bottle: Cut a large opening just below the cap to make a convenient cleaning caddy; stock it with cleaning supplies that you carry from room to room.

Box Tops for Education Seals: Check all of your boxes and labels for a small, rectangular stamp that reads "Box Tops for Education." Clip them and turn them in to your school of choice. Each seal is worth money, which helps schools earn cash for books, computers, playground equipment, and more.

Just remember to strike a balance of sanity with upcycling. We all want to be good to the environment by producing as little waste as possible, but there are recycling facilities or resale establishments like the Salvation Army and Goodwill that will take what we cannot use. It's not necessary to hold onto things that you don't have an immediate or ongoing need for. Do your best to reduce your carbon footprint without increasing your clutter and stress.

Upcycling by Beautifying

The most basic way to upcycle an object is to repair it and restore or improve its beauty. Here are five easy ways to beautify an object and make it new to you.

1. *Decorative Painting.* Apply some metallic trim, an ornate stencil, or an organic design, and you have yourself a showpiece. You don't need a master's degree in fine art and a million hours to get it done. Use patterns, stencils and stamps if you're not confident in your freehand skills. Transfer the patterns to your piece using graphite paper. Tape the graphite paper over the area where you want the image to go, place the image over it, and trace. This will transfer the image onto your item. See chapter four for step-by-step instructions on making a custom stencil. Lastly, buying or making a custom stamp is a method I love to use. It works great on wood and cloth if you're looking for that distressed, shabby chic look. A stamp receives and absorbs paint unevenly, so when transferred to the surface, the image is often thin or speckled and transparent in areas. Don't try to restamp; just fill in these areas by hand if you want.

2. *Apply an Alternative Surface.* A tabletop that's rough, cracked, or warped can be remedied simply by covering it. If you're looking for something substantial and permanent, you'll want to lay down a new surface. This can be as simple as gluing down a game board or mirror (custom glass shops often cut mirrors to an exact size if you need this done).

I wanted a game table for my living room. As I shopped around for one, I discovered they were really difficult to find and cost upwards of five hundred dollars. So I approached this process in reverse. I had the solution of adding a chessboard to a tabletop, and then in someone's trash, I found a deplorable table that I was able to fix up with paint and cover the top with the chessboard.

3. *Cover With Fabric.* Fabric hides problem areas and adds to the décor. Small damage, like chips or water stains, are easy to cover with an embroidered doily. Embroidering doesn't necessarily mean kitschy ribbons and roses. There are all sorts of patterns. You can even create your own by tracing a foam stamp with a fabric pencil to transfer it.

A time-saving alternative would be to sew a punchy print fabric into a dresser scarf or table runner. Or trim a silk scarf with lace or pom-pom

How to Make a Custom Stamp

MATERIALS

Printed image or design	Cardboard
Glue stick	Paint
Foam paper (craft foam sheets)	Paint brush or roller
Craft knife	

1. Select an image or pattern that can be simplified into a silhouette. Print it on paper and cut it out.

2. Use a glue stick to adhere your image onto foam paper.

3. With a craft knife, cut out the silhouette. Remove the paper cut out.

4. Glue the foam stamp onto the cardboard. Be sure to glue it in reverse of how you want it to appear on your furniture or fabric. Hold it up in front of a mirror to make sure everything looks the way you want it to. Trim the cardboard closely around the foam image. This will make it easier to see where you are placing the image.

5. Give the stamp adequate paint coverage. If it's a large surface, you may want to use a small paint roller. Be sure the paint doesn't dry in areas before you're finished painting the whole piece.

6. When applying the stamp to your surface, hold the stamp out about an inch for visual positioning. Then drop or quickly push it onto the surface. This will prevent you from slipping or wiggling the stamp on the surface.

Decorative stamp placed on a pillow using fabric paint.

fringe. In addition to covering problem areas and adding visual interest to a room, the fabric minimizes the appearance of dust, a nice bonus.

4. *Disguise With Decorative Duct Tape.* Yes, re-cover your furniture with decorative duct tape. I have truly never experienced such instant gratification as taping over damaged wood. Just pick your project and start stretching out strips of tape. You can wrap it around legs and rungs. Hold down a warped piece of veneer. Conceal gouges and imperfections while increasing sturdiness and aesthetics. It's also a worry-free process. There is no spilling, dripping, or kicking over messy liquids like paint, varnish, or glue. And if you make a mistake, pull it up and reapply. Read between the lines and you'll hear me saying, "Let your kids do this project." I was able to confidently walk away and let my third grader take over without fear of accidents.

You can choose from a wide variety of prints that work well together. Try mixing and matching. If you want your money to go further, pick solid colors. They come in twenty-yard rolls for typically the same price as the ten-yard print rolls. Either way you go, you'll be left with a great looking "new" piece.

Add a new surface, such as a game board, to cover blemishes on tables.

Embroider fabric with a cute or funky pattern to make a doily that quickly and easily covers small imperfections on surfaces.

5. *Use Mod Podge.* If you're looking to get major flare from bold and intricate prints, use Mod Podge to apply to-die-for fabrics and decorative paper. It makes for a stellar contrast to solid paint.

The trick with Mod Podge is to have everything prepared when you start your project. If your material is somewhat see-through, you'll want the surface underneath it to be a light color so your finished look isn't compromised by background noise. Have your surface clean, precut your fabric or paper (I suggest allowing for extra length and width on fabric because it can be trimmed off afterward or folded over edges), and keep your craft knife and smoothing tool handy. Generously apply the Mod Podge to the area you want to cover. Foam brushes work great for this application. Immediately place your fabric or paper. After you lay down your material, carefully work out any wrinkles. The best smoothing tools I've found are plastic spackle applicators and stiff gift cards (the ones that resemble credit cards). Push your material out toward the edges, making sure it's completely flat. After your material is in place, use your craft knife to trim the edges. When the material is dry, apply a final coat of Mod Podge over

This piano bench was recovered with Duck Tape brand duct tape in Midnight and Houndstooth and Zig-Zag Zebra patterns.

the top to seal it. Voila! To watch a video on this buffet table project visit: www.youtube.com/TheEveOfReduction.

Transformers

Do you drool over a catalog from IKEA or The Container Store? Everything is so neat and organized in beautiful containers on shiny new shelves. It's true, shelves and containers make it so much easier to organizer, but it's not true that you need to run out and buy the latest and greatest containers and shelves to organize in an attractive and functional way. You can create your own custom shelves, containers, and extra storage through the magic of upcycling. Transforming old furniture into new, inventive pieces is fun, inexpensive (sometimes completely free), and good for the environment.

Buffet, before

Buffet, after. Apply decorative fabric or paper using Mod Podge for exquisite visual appeal.

In this section, I'll show you how to transform easy-to-find furniture pieces into items that help you organize your home. If you don't have a spare dresser, headboard, wooden chair, or coffee table around your house, don't worry. These items are easy to find curb side or in thrift stores (I'll explain how to find items in these locations later in the chapter). I guarantee you'll feel great when you see a former piece of clutter being used to help organize your home.

PROJECT 1:

Closet Organizers Made From Dresser Tops and Drawer Fronts

Step back, expensive closet organizational systems and flimsy wire racks. You can create your own closet organizer using an old dresser. Narrower drawer fronts can serve as a panel for hooks, and this panel can be mounted to your wall. Larger drawer fronts and dresser tops make excellent shelving.

The façade of a dresser holds its best assets. This is where you'll find sturdy, quality wood, even if it's glued to cheap particleboard drawers.

The dresser drawers I used for this project were garbage picked in a small town about an hour from my home. The wood was so beautiful that I couldn't pass it up, even though there was no room in my sedan for the entire dresser. Yes, I was forced into a roadside dismantling as dictated by my trunk space. Don't walk away from potential just because it's incomplete. Parts are parts, and they can be just as useful and oftentimes more creatively malleable.

MATERIALS

Drill	Saw (hand or power)
Hammer	Tape measure
Screws and screwdriver	Pencil
Shelf brackets	Stud finder
Coat hooks	

1. Remove the drawer fronts from the rest of the drawer by separating the dovetails, pulling out staples, unscrewing screws, or sawing.

2. To add hooks to a narrow drawer front, decide how many hooks you want on the panel. Use a tape measure and pencil to mark where each hook will be placed. Drill holes where you want to place the hooks and then attach the hooks.

3. Transform larger drawer fronts and dresser tops into shelves. First measure your closet space. Then measure and cut the drawer fronts to fit the space.

4. Use L-brackets to attach the drawer fronts to the wall as shelves. You can find L-brackets with built-in holders for clothes bars at hardware stores. To ensure stability, screw your L-brackets into a wall stud. Wall studs are the support beams behind drywall. Studs are spaced 16" (41cm) apart, so once you find one, it's easy to find others on the same wall.

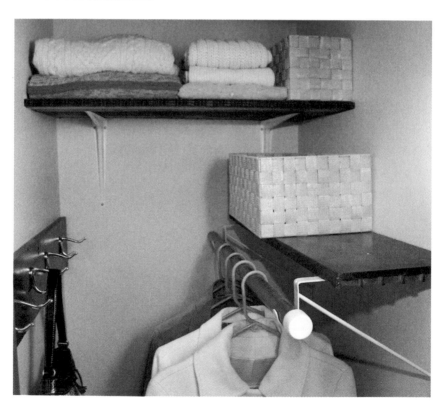

PROJECT 2:
Under-the-Bed Storage Containers
Made From Dresser Drawers

Space can be wasted in two ways: clutter and nothingness. Under the bed is useful, hidden square footage that often goes unused. With three beds in my house, I calculated ninety-six square feet of unused space. How much space do you have that could be appropriated for storage? How would using this space benefit your other storage areas?

It can be hard to access items under the bed, but the right containers make it easy to store and reach items. And once again, you don't need to run out and buy new under-the-bed storage containers. This project shows you how to repurpose dresser drawers as under-the-bed storage containers complete with casters (wheels that pivot and turn in any direction).

Casters will add a few inches (or centimeters) of height to your storage drawers, so be sure you have enough clearance when choosing the drawers you are going to use. If space is tight, you can buy bed risers at a hardware or big-box store to gain a few more inches under your bed. This is also a project where you will want sturdy, well-crafted drawers.

MATERIALS

Drill

4 casters that attach with nuts and
    bolts

4 nuts and bolts

Pencil

Duct tape

Shelf liner (optional)

Labeling supplies like stickers
    or stencils

There are two types of casters: ones that attach with a shaft that is inserted into your furniture, and ones that attach with a metal platform with holes for nuts and bolts. Choose the casters with the metal platform because you are attaching them to a thin piece of wood.

Before

1. Flip your drawer over so the bottom is up. Place a caster in a corner of the drawer. Use your pencil to mark the holes in the caster platform on the drawer bottom. Remove the caster from the drawer.

2. Use your drill to create holes where you placed pencil marks.

3. Line up the holes on your caster with the holes in your drawer and screw them in place with the nuts and bolts. Add bolts from inside the drawer and secure them with the nuts on the bottom of the drawer to keep them in place.

4. The bolt heads will stick out on the inside of your drawer. Cover them with a piece of duct tape so they don't damage the contents of your drawer. To further protect items, you can add shelf liner to the drawers.

5. Repeat steps 1–4 to attach the other three casters, one in each corner of the drawer.

6. Finish it up by labeling your drawer's contents on the drawer front with stencils or stickers, or by decorating with Mod Podge.

   If you're concerned about dust collecting in an open drawer, you can easily top it with a piece of cardboard. For a permanent solution, use a shelf hinge to attach a piece of wood, cut to the same size as the drawer's footprint. If you're really thinking like an upcycler, use an old game board or the bottom from another drawer as a lid.

Under-the-bed storage drawers

Alternative Project

If you have a narrow but deep drawer, you could upcycle it into a storage ottoman. Add the casters as directed above or add short, wooden legs. Attach a hinged top that is covered with batting and fabric for a comfy, attractive footrest or seat.

Kitchen Island Made From a Dresser

I've never met a kitchen that couldn't use more food-preparation surface and extra storage. Kitchen islands add both, but they can be expensive, and sometimes there's no room—unless you make one yourself. Put it on wheels and you can use it as extra surface area in the dinning room when entertaining or store it in another room when not in use if it doesn't fit in the kitchen. An old dresser is the bones to your new kitchen island.

Naturally, the top of your dresser is not going to be an ideal prep area, so you'll want to add a proper kitchen surface like butcher block, tile, Formica, or granite. Shop construction outlet stores in your area for contractor left-overs. For my island, I chose to cover the surface with small glass tile, which I also used on my drawers to cover holes left from the original decorative metal details that I removed. A kitchen island is also a great starter project for learning how to install tile—it's small, flat, and doesn't get walked on. In other words, it's a best-case-scenario application to get a feel for the materials and process used in tiling.

Most short dressers are 3" to 5" (7cm to 12cm) shorter than the standard kitchen island. We'll make up that height by adding wood beams and casters to the bottom of the dresser. The wood beams will allow an open shelf to be attached beneath the dresser. This shelf is the perfect storage space for large, awkward kitchen supplies like your electric griddle, cutting board, and cookie sheets.

Other augmentations you could add are hooks for utensils and pot-holders, a towel bar, paper towel holder, can opener, and bottle opener.

MATERIALS

Paint (color of your choice)

Intact dresser (the dresser I used measures 19"d × 44"w × 32"h [48cm d × 112cm w × 81cm h])

Kitchen-friendly surface, such as butcher block, granite, or tile

Plywood, measuring the width of the dresser legs from left to right, by the measured distance inside the dresser legs from front to back. For me that was 38"w × 14"d (97cm w × 36cm d).

2, 2" (5cm) beams of wood the length
of the dresser legs from front to
back. Height will be judged on
how much you want to raise your
kitchen island.

4, 1" (25mm) nails

4 screws

4 casters with shafts

Screwdriver

Paintbrush

Drill

Rubber mallet

Pencil

Wood glue

Dust mask

Thinset

V-notch trowel

Unsanded grout

Sponge

Grout float

Drawer dividers

New hardware, hooks, magnetic strip,
paper towel holder, can opener
(optional accessories)

1. Use a screwdriver to remove the old hardware from your dresser. Prep it and paint it your desired color.

2. Position your plywood so each end is centered over a 2" (5cm) beam. It should look like a capital letter "I" lying horizontal. Nail the plywood to the beams.

3. Flip your dresser over so it is standing on its top with the legs in the air. Place your wood beams on top of the legs so the plywood is running the width of the dresser. Drill screw holes through the beams and into the dresser legs. Screw the beams into the dresser legs. The plywood will create an open shelf at the bottom of the dresser between the dresser legs.

4. Use your drill to drill tap holes through the beams. Position your caster holes just to the outside of the screws that attach the beams to the dresser legs. The caster holes should be slightly smaller than the caster shaft's circumference and the same length as the caster's shaft.

5. Drop a small amount of wood glue into the hole and use a rubber mallet to tap the caster's shaft tight into the tap hole. Repeat steps 4 and 5 for the other three casters.

6. Flip your dresser upright to begin preparing the dresser top for a new surface (in my case, glass tile installation). Clean your dresser top to prepare it to receive the new surface.

7. Arrange your tiles. Most likely, the mosaic tile sheets you purchased will be backed in mesh. Lay out the sheets, cutting and arranging for full coverage of your dresser top. Rotate your tile sheets so the cut mesh always faces inward and the outer edge has no mesh netting sticking out. Move the sheets to a near-by location where they can remain in their proper arrangement.

8. Put on a dust mask and then mix and spread your adhesive mortar made of cement (Thinset). You'll mix the powder substance with water until it's the consistency of toothpaste. In your mixing tray, use your V-notch trowel to test the thickness. You want to be sure that when you run the notched edge through the mortar, it will hold its shape, but not be too stiff. Spread the mortar on evenly over your dresser top. With the notched edge of the trowel comb at a 45-degree angle to achieve a thickness of ⅛" (3mm). Immediately wipe up any mortar that may have dripped.

9. Carefully place your tile sheets over the mortar. Wipe around the edges in case any mortar oozed out. Let it sit to harden for at least 24 hours before applying the grout.

10. Mix the unsanded grout with water until it reaches the same consistency as your adhesive mortar. Let it sit while you wet the tiles with a sponge. Apply the grout over the tiles with a grout float. Work the grout between the tiles in a vertical and horizontal motion. Run the grout float diagonally to remove excess grout. Using a damp sponge, wipe clean the tile faces. Let the grout sit for at least forty-eight hours.

11. Add hardware (new or old) to the drawers and add optional accessories as desired.

Dresser, before (top) and finished kitchen island (above)

How to Add Drawer Dividers

Kitchen items are small and numerous. To keep them well organized and handy, it helps to install drawer dividers.

MATERIALS

Wood scraps ½" (13mm) thick	T square
Tape measure	Jigsaw
Pencil	Wood glue

1. Select wood scraps you may have, or purchase some from a home improvement store. Wood should be about ½" (13mm) thick.

2. Measure the width and depth of your drawer. Draw your drawer divider layout on paper to give yourself a working guide. Consider space for all of your supplies: towels, aprons, cookbooks, potholders, and utensils.

3. Using a pencil and T square, mark the cutting lines in your wood. Cut with a jigsaw.

4. To give a clean look, paint the exposed, cut edges to match the outside of your island.

5. Secure the dividers in the drawer with wood glue.

Drawer with added dividers

Bench Made From a Headboard and Coffee Table

Benches can be used throughout your house, but are especially functional in your outdoor living space and entryways where you put on and take off shoes. Use benches instead of chairs to get more seating around your dining room table for large gatherings. They're extremely versatile and easy to construct when starting with a headboard and coffee table. The headboard is the backrest, while the coffee table is the seat.

MATERIALS

Headboard	Screwdriver
Coffee table	Sandpaper
Jigsaw	Primer
Duct tape	Paint
Drill	Paintbrush
2 utilitarian L-brackets	Wood glue (optional)
6, 1" (25mm) screws	Craft sticks (optional)
2, 3" (76mm) screws	

1. Saw off the legs of the headboard, leaving the headboard the desired height for the bench's backrest. To help ensure the cuts are straight, I wrap a piece of duct tape around the leg to mark a straight line. I cut one leg and then hold it even with the other leg (keeping it in place with my hand) to mark a matching cutting line.

2. When both legs are cut, stand the headboard on the coffee table to test how it sits. You may need to shave off or sand down one side so it sits flat and level on the table-top. Tip: If you do notice a slight angle in your cut, you can use wood glue and craft sticks to even it off. Fill in any gaps with wood filler before you paint (step 5).

3. Situate the headboard on the coffee table and mark the screw holes for the metal L-brackets on the end posts of the headboard. There should be two screw holes on each side of the bracket. Insert a 1" (25mm) screw into each of the vertical holes (the ones going into the back side of the headboard).

4. The bracket is going to extend under the bottom of the coffee table. The first horizontal hole on the bracket will be positioned under both the coffee table top and the bottom of the headboard posts (where you sawed). Insert a 3" (76mm) screw into

this hole, drilling all the way through the tabletop and into the headboard. This is crucial to the bench's stability.

5. After the two pieces are securely joined, prime and paint your bench. This is where your piece goes from Frankenstein to fabulous. Oh, and some handmade throw pillows can really help with the wow factor.

Headboard, before

Coffee table, before

The finished bench

PROJECT 5:

Message Board Made From a Window Shutter

Life is busy. There are appointments, mail, permission slips, raffle tickets, and coupons to keep in order. A centralized information center in the home helps everyone's days run smoothly. It's time everyone gets in the loop. A message board in a high-traffic area of your home is a perfect organization and communication solution, and an old window shutter can bring it all together.

For this project, I used a polymer window shutter, which is lightweight, durable, and comes with predrilled holes that can be used for adding hooks or knobs.

MATERIALS

Polymer window shutter	Hooks
Cork	Drawer pulls and rubber faucet
Cardboard	washers
Craft glue	Drill
Tracing paper	Screws
Crafter's plywood	Stud finder
Craft knife	Screwdriver
Chalkboard spray-paint	Pencil
Wood glue	Level

1. Paint your shutter if desired.

2. Use tracing paper to create a template for the curved areas in the shutter. Use the template to cut the cork and a matching cardboard piece. For added stability and depth for your push pins, glue the cork onto the cardboard backing.

3. Using a craft knife, trim crafter's plywood to fit the shutter recess. Paint the plywood with chalkboard paint. (I used three coats of spray-paint.)

4. Apply wood glue to the shutter area where you are dropping in the cork and chalkboard pieces.

5. Attach metal strips and hooks or drawer pulls as desired. If you're using drawer pulls, you'll need to add two to three rubber faucet washers to screw them in tight because they're going through thin plastic. Golf tees and a bit of wood glue also work great for filling the shutter's predrilled holes. See the Surfaces for Message Board sidebar for more on each type of material.

Surfaces for a Message Board

Customize your message board by selecting materials that fit your needs and style. Use a variety of materials to make your surface versatile. Here are some options:

1. *Cork:* You can pick up rolls or sheets of cork at a craft store and cut it to fit your desired space or cut it into a decorative shape. It's also helpful to have cork because thumbtacks can handle your heavier things like calendars and multipage phone lists.

2. *Chalkboard:* Chalkboard paint is easily accessible. You can apply the paint to precut plexiglass or crafter's plywood that can attach to the shutter.

3. *Metal strip:* Including a metal strip on your message board gives you the flexibility and ease of using magnets on it. You can attach a magnetic strip (available at craft stores) to all kinds of things you want to keep handy—pens, chip clips, and containers for paper clips and chalk.

4. *Hooks or pulls:* You may want to make your shutter a dual-purpose message board and coat rack. This will definitely draw attention to your communication center. Family members will pause to put on their coats and simultaneously be reminded of things they need to take with them when they leave the house for the day. Hooks can be used for hanging storage organizers and keys, too. Storage containers can be as simple as hanging aluminum cans or repurposing packaging, such as sidewalk chalk pails.

6. Drill holes in your shutter, 32" (81cm) apart.

7. Use a stud finder and mark the stud. Hold your message board up to the wall and decide at what height you want to hang it (you may need a partner for this). Use a level to ensure it's straight. Mark the screw holes in pencil.

8. Drill directly into the wall where you marked and screw in your message board.

The finished message board

Curtain Holdbacks Made From Headboard Finials

When it comes to upcycling an item, I'm a big fan of considering all of the item's parts. Sometimes the smallest parts are the only salvageable things or all that will fit your needs. Such was the case when I garbage-picked a damaged headboard years ago. The effort it would have taken to restore the headboard far outweighed my need or desire for it. At the time, I was installing drapes to minimize the opening between my living room and dining room, and I wanted something elegant but not too obstructive to help tie them back.

I sawed off the headboard finials, spray-painted them gold, and attached them to my wall. They're kind of like a riddle now. It's fun to show them to people and let them guess what they were.

Keep in mind that, the method of mounting I use for these finials can be applied to other surfaces that fit flush with your wall, such as mounting a wooden box or crate used for shelving.

MATERIALS

Headboard finial	Drill
Jigsaw	8 screws
Duct tape	4 screw anchors
Spray-paint	4 small, flush mount picture hangers

1. Use a jigsaw to saw off the finials on the headboard. To help ensure the cuts are straight, I wrap a piece of duct tape around the finial to mark a straight line. I cut one finial and then hold it even with the other finial to mark a matching cutting line.

2. Paint the finial using the color of your choice. Spray-paint is a quick, easy solution for these small items.

3. To attach the wooden finials to your wall, hold one flush mount to the wall and trace the two screw holes on the wall. Drill your marked holes and insert your screw anchors. Screw in the flush mount with the "fingers" facing upward.

4. Repeat Step 3 on the finial, except attach the flush mount with the "fingers" facing down, as shown in the inset picture.

5. Slide the finial mount down onto the mount on the wall.

6. Repeat for the second finial.

The finished curtain holdback

Five Other Repurposes for Finials

I realize curtain holdbacks are kind of a specific need. So if that isn't on your to-do list, here are five other ways to repurpose finials.

1. *Furniture legs:* Finials are often very decorative and sturdy, and therefore work well as short furniture legs. Attach them directly to an ottoman, couch or box spring.

2. *Chair embellishment:* I'm all for taking a lackluster piece of furniture and dressing it up with some repurposed details. A boring chair can gain a bunch of respect when fitted with some fancy finials. Attach the finials to the top corners of the chair back.

3. *Knobs:* Before you go out and buy a post or hook to hang your bathrobe on, what about using a finial? If you have small finials, they can live on as drawer pulls.

4. *Hose guides:* Have you ever yanked the garden hose causing it to karate-chop your flower bed? Avoid the massacre by installing hose guides. You'll need to find (or buy) something for the base that will stick into the ground and fit into the base of your finial. Metal pipes or the mattress support bars on the bottom of a crib work great. Find instructions for how to make hose guides at http://eveofreduction.blogspot.com/2012/07/upcycle-crib-to-hose-guides.html

5. *Curtain rod finials:* Well, we're back to curtains. A makeshift curtain rod (think PVC pipe) can be easily camouflaged by decorating the ends with finials. If you're having trouble attaching the rod and the finials, try screwing a cork to the bottom of the finials and inserting the cork into the hollow rod.

PROJECT 7:
Coffee Table Made From a Door and Chair

Lay down an old door and you have a substantial tabletop. This project combines chair legs with a door to create a coffee table. Chairs are easy to come by for free. I find oddball chairs that are in all states of disrepair everywhere.

A great feature of a door coffee table is not only its ample size, but the open space underneath that makes it comfortable to sit around. If you live in a home without a dining room or in a studio apartment where you need your space to be multifunctional, a door coffee table can double as a casual eating area. Just add some throw pillows around it! It can also function in your outdoor space as a place to set out food (think buffet style) or make it the kid's table.

MATERIALS

Wooden door	Pencil
Wooden chair	Wood glue
Jigsaw	Sandpaper
Tape measure	Drill
Paint	4 screws
Paintbrush	Screwdriver

1. To salvage chair legs for the purpose of table legs, we're going to keep them attached to the chair seat. The chair seat must be flat without any teetering when it rests on the door. Saw off or unscrew the chair back where it attaches to the seat.

2. Measure the width of the seat surface and draw a pencil line to mark the exact center.

3. Use your jigsaw to cut down the center of the seat. You want to split the chair in half. Completely saw off any connecting rungs that run between the two pieces you're dividing. Paint the chair seat halves and the door

4. Determine where you want to position your chair legs. I measured the length of my table, divided that in to quarters and then centered the chair halves at the ¼ and ¾ increments.

5. Drill screw holes through the bottom of the chair seat.

6. Sand the flat areas of the chair seat and the underside of the door where you're going to glue the pieces together. Clean and dry the sanded area. Trace the chair seat onto the bottom side of the door so you know exactly where to apply the wood glue. Be sure to spread the glue over the entire surface within your outlined boundaries.

7. Secure the chair to the door with two screws on each chair half through the predrilled holes from step 5. Repeat steps 6 and 7 for the other half of the chair seat.

8. There will be a doorknob hole in your tabletop. You could glue down a decorative tile to cover the hole or fill the hole with a vase made from an upside-down plastic ketchup bottle or wine bottle. The bottom of the ketchup bottle can easily be removed with a craft knife. See the Wine Bottle Vase sidebar for instructions on making an inverted wine bottle vase.

Additional Table Leg Options

You can transform a door into tables used for work, entertaining, or just resting your feet. The type of legs will determine the function. Possible table legs include:

- legs cut off headboards and footboards
- legs unscrewed from another table
- segments from an old wooden ladder

Finished coffee table (above) and finished wine bottle vase (left)

Wine Bottle Vase

An upcycle option for filling the hole left by the doorknob in your new coffee table is to create a wine bottle vase. If your table is being used as a work area, this vase makes a great no-spill pencil and ruler holder. In this project, you remove the bottom of the bottle so the tapered end fits in the hole.

MATERIALS

Wine bottle

Acetone nail polish remover

100 percent cotton T-shirt

Lighter

Sandpaper

Decorative tape (optional)

Champagne cork or screw-top cap

Safety glasses

Rubber gloves

1. Cut a long, ½" (13mm) thick strip from an old, 100 percent cotton T-shirt. Stretch the strip so the cut edges curl in on each other.

2. Wrap the strip around the bottom of your wine bottle twice, knot it and trim the hanging strings so the strip is smooth and neat.

3. Put on your rubber gloves to keep your hands free from acetone.

4. Remove the strip of T-shirt and thoroughly soak it in acetone.

5. Rewrap the strip around the bottle where you want to cut it. Don't let the strips separate. Instead, the two layers should be right up against each other or twisted together. You want one clean cut.

6. Remove your rubber gloves and put on your safety glasses.

7. Fill a sink or tub with cold water.

8. Hold the wine bottle over the water and light the T-shirt on fire.

9. As the string burns, slowly turn the bottle.

10. As soon as the flame goes out, dunk the bottle immediately in the cold water. The bottom portion will pop off.

11. Sand down the cut-glass ridge at the top of the vase or cover it with a strip of decorative tape.

12. Plug the neck of the bottle with a champagne cork unless the bottle used a screw cap, in which case you can use the cap.

PROJECT 8:

Corner Shelf Made From a Bifold Door

Corner shelves help you maximize space that can be difficult to use. Bifold doors are pretty easy to find because they take a lot of abuse, causing their gliding mechanisms to break while the structure of the door is still fine. Reusing them for stationary purposes, like shelving, is a great alternative to sending them to the dump.

MATERIALS

Bifold door	Level
Screwdriver	2 ½" (64mm) screws
3 or 4 pieces of wood (to be used as shelves)	Drill
	Tape measure
Jigsaw (if shelves need to be cut)	Heavy-gauge wire (like that used for hanging pictures and mirrors)
T square	
Pencil	Furniture tack
Paint in color of your choice	Wall hook
Paintbrush	

Before you start: The back side of the bifold door is sometimes plain (aka, visually uninteresting). If that's the case, remove the hinges, and flip the bifold doors over to the front side. Drill new holes and reattach the hinges to the front so the most attractive side is facing out.

1. For this project, you'll need to source three to four wood shelves. They can be triangles or quarter-circles. Cut your own from an unused tabletop or wooden planks. Use a T square and pencil to measure and draw your cutting lines. If you don't have raw materials to work from, some hardware stores (including big-box hardware stores) will custom cut wood that you purchase in their store.

2. Paint your door and shelves as desired. Remember that the underside of at least the top shelf will be visible due to its positioned height; therefore, you'll want to paint the top and bottom.

3. Use your tape measure to measure where you want to position your shelves. Stand the doors upright and opened flat. Draw a horizontal pencil line across the back side of your doors at each shelf height. Use a level to make sure your line is straight.

4. Drill two holes into the pencil line on each side of the bifold door, going through the door and into your shelf. (Note: The screw holes cannot get too close to the outer edge of the door because the shelves come to a point and they're too shallow there to insert the screw.) Twist in the screws. Repeat this step for each shelf.

5. Because this shelf unit is tall with a small footprint, you may want to child-proof the shelving unit by securing it to the wall so it can't be tipped forward. You can do this with heavy-gauge wire and a wall hook. Tap a small furniture tack into the back of one side of the bifold doors, close to the center bend. Wrap and twist a wire loop around the tack head, leaving enough slack that it can reach a wall hook nailed into the wall opposite the tack. Keep in mind that a baseboard is likely keeping your corner shelf about a ½" (13mm) away from the wall. Your wire loop will need to bridge that gap but still be tight enough to hook tightly onto the wall hook.

Alternative Project

If a corner shelf doesn't work in your space, use the bifold doors for horizontal shelving. Remove the hinges (save them in your Reduction Rebel toolbox for another project). Separately, these doors can provide about thirteen feet of shelving. You could even use a jigsaw to cut the doors to custom fit your wall space (or closet). Just remember, you'll need two L-brackets for every shelf.

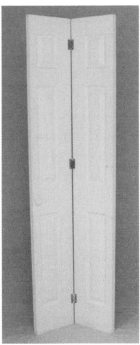

Bifold door before and
Finished corner shelf

Shoe Rack Made From a Crib

Ladies and gentlemen, boys and girls, we have shoes up the ying-yang. And at first glance, you may be thinking of simply having a crib full of shoes. That works, but it's far from organized. That's why we're going to hack up the crib and use its wonderful, wooden slats to make a three-tiered shoe rack. In fact, we can make two shoe racks—one from each crib side. Plus, I'll show you how to make a very basic shoe rack that takes only fifteen minutes to assemble.

Cribs and other baby furniture are pretty easy to find for fair prices. Sellers have no use for them, so they just want to get rid of them. On the other hand, you may find you're in the position of the potential seller and thinking more like, I hate to unload a two-hundred-dollar changing table for twenty-five dollars. Well, you don't have to. You can upcycle it into something you can use on a daily basis.

MATERIALS

Wooden crib	Tape measure
Jigsaw	Sandpaper
Hammer	Wood stain that matches the crib's
1" (25mm) nails	finish
Level	Paintbrush
Pencil	

1. Unscrew or use your jigsaw to detach the slatted sides from the crib. The slats need to remain intact, so cut about 2" (5cm) into the crib base so the sides remain one solid unit.

2. My crib had 15 wooden slats on each side. Working with a single side, I used the jigsaw to cut 5 separate three-slat pieces. All the pieces are the same size.

3. Set aside 2 of the pieces you cut in step 2 as the sides of your rack. Lay these vertically on your work table.

4. The remaining three-slat pieces serve as the horizontal shelves. Lay these horizontally between the 2 vertical pieces in step 3. One shelf will go at the top and another at the bottom. There will be a lip at the top and bottom of the sidepieces that you can

butt the shelves against for added stability. Measure the vertical side and place the center shelf directly in the middle. Use your pencil to mark the correct placement on each side.

5. Neatly hammer small finishing nails (I used 1" [24mm] nails) through the sides and into the shelves to keep it all together. Use a level to ensure the shelves are level.

6. Sand the exposed, cut edges and touch up with matching stain.

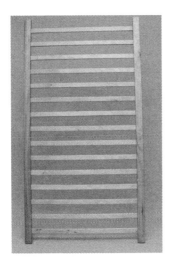

Finished shoe rack

The Fifteen-Minute Shoe Rack

MATERIALS

Entire side of a slatted crib, removed from the crib base

Adhesive-backed Velcro strips

½ yard (46cm) of wool felt cut into 2, 18" (46cm) pieces (approx. 22" × 18" [56cm × 46cm])

1. Turn the side of the crib so the slats are horizontal to the ground. Choose which side of the crib you want facing out. Then position the crib side so the back side is facing you.

2. Stick 3 pieces of adhesive Velcro on the back side of each of the first 4 wood slats (one piece on the left, one center, and one right). Be sure the pieces are spaced no wider than the width of your fabric. Tip: Use the loop side of the Velcro for the crib and the soft side of the Velcro for the felt.

3. On one side of the felt, place a strip of Velcro in the top left, center and right, along the 22" (56cm) side.

4. Flip your felt over and place a strip of Velcro in the bottom left, center and right, along the 22" (56cm) side.

PROJECT 10:

Wine Bar Made From a Changing Table

A changing table is essentially three shelves, so you could just use it as storage and move on with your life. But chances are your changing table has nice wooden details, which means it could have a prominent place in your home. So as life moves from diapers, why not transform your changing table into a drinks station? A wine bar makes for an elegant, functional conversation piece (not to mention conversation port) when it's repurposed from a changing table.

5. To make fabric pockets, hold up your felt so the side with the Velcro on the bottom is facing you and the Velcro at the top is facing the Velcro on the crib piece. Press the Velcro on the fabric into the Velcro on the second slat from the top. Fold the bottom of the felt toward you and press the bottom Velcro into the Velcro on the first wood slat. Repeat this process to make another fabric pocket shelf if you have a lot of sandals and flats.

6. Flip the side of the crib so the fabric pockets are in back. The Velcro side will face the wall. Lean the top end of the crib side against the wall with the bottom about a foot away from the wall. Hang high heels from the remaining slats. To hold sneakers, insert the toes between the slats. Because they're so close together, the slats will hold your shoes.

Finished fifteen-minute shoe rack

MATERIALS

Jigsaw

Wine corks (approximately 400, enough to cover a shelf of the changing table)

Wood glue

2 under-cabinet stemware racks (purchased or assembled from scrap wood)

Short bolts and nuts

Drill

Craft knife

Shipping tube

Tape measure

Pencil

Screwdriver

Mod Podge

Fabric

1. With your jigsaw, remove the front portion of the "fence" that runs around the perimeter of the top shelf of the changing table. This way, the front of your wine bar will be open so bottles and glasses can move in and out freely.

2. Attach the stemware racks to the underside of the changing table's topmost surface. If you bought your stemware rack, it will come with screws. You can save those for another project. You'll need nuts and bolts to secure the rack to the thin top shelf of your changing table. The nuts will be exposed on the top side of your shelf, but don't worry, you'll cover the nuts with wine corks in the next step.

3. Cover the topmost surface with wine corks using wood glue. Assemble the corks into a pattern or design if you wish; corks are easy to cut with a craft knife if you need to fill in smaller gaps in your design. Be sure to dig out a recess in the corks that go over the nuts from the stemware racks so those corks lay flush with the other corks.

4. The lowest shelf is where you'll store your wine bottles. Use a (recycled) shipping tube to make a scalloped holder for your bottles. The one I used was 25" (64cm) long with a circumference of 13" (33cm). Cut the tube in quarters so you have four 6¼" (16cm) tubes. Then make an incision down the length of each tube. Wrap a tape measure around the tube to measure the point exactly half the distance from your incision. Make a second cut to divide the tubes in half lengthwise. You will have 8 semi-cylinders. Lay them on the bottom shelf to see how many will comfortably fit on the shelf before Mod Podging them together. For my changing table, only 7 semi-cylinders fit in the space.

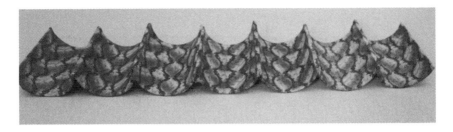

5. Cover the cut tubes with Mod Podge and fabric that will complement your décor. The fabric will bring them together as one scalloped unit. Place a wine bottle in each tube to keep the bottles from rolling around. The tubes also give you a stable base that you can stack additional bottles on top of to make a pyramid.

Some finishing touches could include a wine glass charm holder, corkscrew stand, and ring labels for the necks of your wine bottles.

Changing table, before and finished wine table

Picking With the Lights On

Maybe the projects in this chapter inspired you, but you don't have the raw furniture items in your home. No worries! You can find these items for free in your community. You just need to know where to look.

My husband and I are prolific garbage-pickers. We make no bones about it. We've picked from neighbors, friends, strangers, and estates. But I recognize this may be a new (and possibly unappealing) concept to many people. Let me put you at ease by assuring you that garbage-picking doesn't mean diving head first into someone's trash to dig through their soggy newspapers and moldy leftovers. "Garbage" worth picking is out in the open, either in boxes or open bins or freestanding.

Believe it or not, there is an etiquette to garbage-picking, and if you follow these guidelines, both you and any homeowners you encounter will have pleasant picking experiences.

First, just relax and leave your embarrassment at home. You're doing this in the name of creativity, thrift, and Mother Earth. Besides, people love to know their stuff is going to someone who appreciates it and can use it. If you see the homeowner outside, don't be afraid to pull up and confirm the curb-side heap is available by giving a friendly, "Hi, do you mind if I take a look?" Ask, "Is this stuff you're getting rid of?" Or try a specific question like, "Is this a sewing cabinet?" It may sound rhetorical, but it breaks the ice and keeps you from looking like a trespasser. Be friendly, respectful, and curious. I call this basic picking etiquette.

Picker's Etiquette

1. Be friendly: If homeowners are outside say, "Hello," and if you're in your own neighborhood, introduce yourself.
2. Be respectful: When you're on someone else's property, remember to keep quiet, refrain from making comments, and leave the trash pile tidy.
3. Be curious: When you're passing by a large pile of items on the curb, take the time to investigate. You never know what you'll discover or when inspiration may strike.

While out riding my bicycle one day, I stopped to browse a promising pile and snag some hardware off a set of drawers. The homeowner came out and started talking to me while I was removing the hardware. I admit, I felt very awkward. However, during our conversation, I noticed a black vinyl portfolio in one of his trash cans. It was oddly shaped, so I asked if it was for an instrument. As it turns out, it was for an archery bow. Bingo. Rewind a couple of chapters and you'll remember

> People love to know their stuff is going to someone who appreciates it and can use it.

I'm an archer. I would never have investigated if I had bolted when I saw the homeowner coming out of the house (which was my initial reaction). The kicker was that the homeowner ran back inside and grabbed fifteen pristine arrows for me that only needed new flights. These arrows were super-sharp and could kill a wild boar. Certainly he didn't feel comfortable putting deadly weapons in his trash, but to the right picker, it was open season.

Who knows what other treasures people are harboring? With a little chitchat, you could build enough rapport to foster unexpected generosity. Don't be surprised to meet new neighbors, fellow hobbyists, or just helpful souls along the way. There will be those who give you information, like, "This is a solid maple bed frame," or help you load their stuff into your car. They may even tip you off that more is coming the following week. Let yourself be open to the abundance. Everyone walks away feeling good.

Finding the Sweet Spots

I call a garbage pile with quality pickable items a sweet spot. When considering your target neighborhoods, don't automatically go for the mansions. Bigger houses don't necessarily equate to better garbage. Not that you can't score a sweet piece on Pill Hill. I'm just saying that all neighborhoods, regardless of income level, hold equal opportunity for treasures.

Here are some tips to finding neighborhoods with ample sweet spots.

Know the pickup regulations. Save yourself time by researching collection days and rules. Check the city website or call the municipality. Some communities have strict garbage pickup rules, and homeowners are limited to what they can fit in their trash cans. Ninety-nine percent of the time, these neighborhoods are a complete waste of time. But once or twice a year, they might have an amnesty day when people can throw out anything they want, regardless of size and weight. If you find a community like this, find out when the amnesty days are and mark your calendar. That trash day will contain a guaranteed mother lode of stuff people have been waiting all year to get rid of.

Look for neighborhoods with high turnover rates. Ask your local real estate agents. They know the hot spots for transplants and upgraders. These people are going to dump their stuff at the curb on their way out.

Watch for garage sales. They'll be listed in your weekly paper (the one that's free) or on Craigslist. You'll also see signs nailed to telephone poles and taped to stop signs. Hit up the neighborhood on the trash day following the sale. People often simply toss unsold items. I've picked many perfectly good items that still had the price tag from the garage sale.

> The holidays parade in with new TVs, recliners, curio cabinets, and bedroom sets. Out with the old, in with the new. This is prime time for the enterprising and informed.

Watch for seasonal clean-outs. Correctly timing seasonal clean-outs simply takes some common sense. Was there just a burst of warm weather in March? After months of cabin fever, homeowners get the itch to clean house. Is a major holiday coming up? People will be in the final push to get their houses presentable before crowds of company come for the holidays. And not only are they sprucing up the place and purging unwanted items, they're expecting more. Yes, the holidays parade in with new TVs, recliners, curio cabinets, and bedroom sets. Out with the old, in with the new. This is prime time for the enterprising and informed. Get out there and reap the rewards.

How to Identify What Is Worth Picking

You can upcycle anything, but some items and materials have more potential than others. Some items, like coffee makers, hockey skates, flat-screen monitors, and patio furniture, will require minor repairs or cleaning and be as good as new for use in your home or for sale online. Other items, such as dressers, computer desks, or lone chairs, may have great "bones"—raw materials that can be taken apart and used in a new way.

Anything made of wood or metal can be picked for raw materials. Here's how to identify the solid, quality pieces worth taking home versus the flimsy pieces that should be left on the curb.

Wood

Quality wooden items that are worth upcycling will have

- dovetailed joints (two pieces joined together using interlocking teeth, cut in a trapezoid shape)
- joints held together with dowels and screws

Cheap (and possibly flimsy) wooden pieces will use glue or staples at the joints. Cheap doesn't mean it can't be useful. Go ahead and give it the ungraceful test: yank open the drawers. Do they glide? Are they flush? Do they pull out entirely from the unit? Remember to bring a flashlight and a screwdriver. There may not be anything worth your while except the hardware.

Metal

Rust can always be sanded, and chipped paint can be covered. Be on the lookout for bent or broken spots that can cause injury. Unless you're equipped for welding, you might want to take a pass. Or you can make some

Scrap Metal Payout

There is money to be made in recycling scrap metal if you keep the "it all adds up" mentality. Keep in mind, the price of metal fluctuates, so here's a loose guide to give you an idea of the kind of money you're looking at when you scavenge for scrap metal. It's best to check with metal recycling facilities to confirm what they accept and what they buy. For example, a VCR can be recycled, but it has no cash value.

Washing machine $12

Hub cap 10¢

Shopping cart $0 (stolen)

Aluminum screen door $8

coin at a scrap metal recycling facility. Hauling metal to be recycled can earn you some extra cash, but assess if it's worth your while before you embark on the venture.

Upholstered and Stuffed Items
Don't give up on the old upholstered items in your home. You might be able to restuff them or reupholster them to make them new to you for a fraction of the cost of a brand-new item.

However, if you are garbage picking, proceed with caution when it comes to soft goods like couches and fully upholstered chairs. And by all means, stay clear of mattresses. Cushions and fabrics are breeding grounds for germs and bugs, which you definitely don't want to welcome into your home. Not worth it. But if it's something you can easily reupholster, like a removable seat cushion on a wooden chair, load 'er up. Bottom line, if an item is stuffed or has absorbent materials, be sure you can replace these features before taking the item from the garbage.

On the Second Hand

Yes, part of being resourceful is not relying on retail convenience, but when your upcycling needs are a little more specific and your time is limited, you'll want to cut to the chase and head for more predictable hot spots for deals: secondhand retailers. I'm talking about flea markets, consignment shops, thrift stores, garage sales, and estate sales. This includes single-item outlets like the *Penny Saver* and Craigslist, too. They usually include a picture, so you can get a good idea about the item for sale before trekking out to have a look. And although you can definitely get lucky at an auction, auctions aren't at the top of my list because they lack the elements of surprise, brevity (there's no in-and-out with auctions), and negotiating. So while it wouldn't hurt to test the auction waters, I'm going to stick to places where you're the one in control.

Rule number one in any shopping arena is to go in with a game plan. Have a solid idea of what you need, what size will work, and what really tickles your fancy. It's easy to get distracted and come home with a bunch

Have a solid idea of what you need, what size will work, and what really tickles your fancy.

of unique clutter. Keep yourself focused with only a hairline of wiggle room on extras. You'll know what's right when you see it. There is no need to rush because you're not going to die without that exact coffee table. There will always be another sale. Take it in stride and enjoy the ride.

Rule number two is to exercise your bargaining rights. Carefully evaluate the quality of the item. Sure, you want to get a feel for if it really has good bones, but you also want to be able to say, "I noticed there isn't a complete set," or "These legs are a bit wobbly," or "An animal chewed the table leg over here." Your careful observations will help you get the best price. Also, wear your poker face. Breaking into an end-zone dance when you find something you've been looking for forever will not play in your favor when you start to negotiate. Play it cool and always be prepared to walk away.

Rule number three is to time your visit right. Other thrifters will recommend you get there at the crack of dawn. I'm not one of them. Why?

Six Steps for Secondhand Shopping Success

1. Have a list of specific things you need.
2. Measure twice, buy once. Always know the space you have to fit the item you're looking for. Then bring a tape measure so you can find the perfect fit.
3. Bring a flashlight to check closely for imperfections or damage. This will keep you from purchasing junk or give you better leverage in negotiating a deal.
4. Bring a smile. Vendors appreciate customers who are polite and respectful. Believe me, charm can go a long way.
5. Carry small bills. Don't expect vendors to break a twenty-dollar bill at every purchase. Things run smoothly when you don't have to rely on vendors for change.
6. Bring a sturdy tote, wagon, or wheeled cart.

Because I'm not a big fan of competition. It makes you eager, hasty, and more likely to jump on something you're lukewarm about because you think someone else is going to take it from under you. You don't need the pressure. If you're naturally an early riser, then by all means get there early; otherwise there is no need to get crazy. Plus, the deals get better later in the day as sellers become more desperate to get rid of things. The final day of an estate sale typically sports prices that have been slashed by one-third. That's when you can buy a perfectly good refrigerator for 165 dollars and an armchair for fifty dollars.

> Consumerism is an entirely modern development, so the assertion that it is "unchangeable" is utterly silly.

Along with timing your visit right, take your time during your visit so you can take in everything that is for sale. Look through everything at a garage sale. At an estate sale, investigate the less desirable spaces in the home, like the basement, attic, garage, and porch. Also be aware of the wallflowers of the room—the drapes and throw rugs and other items that blend in with the home. Sellers and fellow buyers often overlook these things, and you can get great prices on the nonfeatured items that might take a little more gumption to uncover.

Changing Attitudes

We adapt and that is why we survive. The WWII generation grew victory gardens in response to the food rations. Our generation is beginning to formulate our own course of action against conditions like global warming, foreign oil dependency, and the imbalance of our imports to exports. The culture of reuse is gaining an economic stronghold. EBay is already recycling millions of pounds worth of goods, profiting all who are involved. And car commercials are putting their focus on pre-owned sales and longevity.

Some have the attitude that our patterns of capitalism and consumerism will never change. They think our economy depends on it. The truth is that consumerism is an entirely modern development, so the assertion that it is "unchangeable" is utterly silly.

I see this change already in motion. For some, it's a lifestyle choice, politically motivated by a desire to step more lightly on the earth. For others, it's simply a way of saving money. For those who have very little money, it's a lifesaver.

Fixing broken items, drinking from a reusable bottle rather than a disposable water bottle, and shopping at yard sales has a different posture about it. These aren't the repellent signs of poverty. They're the signs of valuing and respecting both financial and environmental resources.

6: Doing Trumps Having

We all need satisfaction. But where do we go to get it? The mall? That is only a temporary fix until the credit card statement arrives or you lose your newest buy in the pile of stuff you already have. Events, people, and really cool, new products can't make you what you want to be. They simply stir up an emotion. They flatter, inspire, and entertain, but that's all external. True satisfaction is not outside us; it can only be found within.

When do you find yourself looking for cookies, biting your nails, or flipping channels? When you're bored, right? You need some kind of stimulation to satisfy you. In this chapter, I'm going to challenge you to find your satisfaction by identifying your passions and then acting on them. This is living life to the fullest instead of passing time and relying on outside stimulants, specifically consuming (be it merchandise or food). Being productive satisfies our need for indulging.

We will look at things and how they come into our lives—that says a lot about our character. We will manifest the emotions and talents inside ourselves to live a life of abundance without maintenance, fear, and monotony.

Doing Without Improves Your Consumer Experiences

Have you ever wondered how people who have so much can be miserable? It's all a matter of perspective. What we lack is easily noticed—especially if it's something we need, like a drink on a hot, sunny day. When we receive what we lack, we welcome it. When we lack nothing, we can't welcome anything new into our lives. In fact, instead of welcoming objects, we either disregard them or feel burdened by them because we have excess.

> We will manifest the emotions and talents inside ourselves to live a life of abundance without maintenance, fear, and monotony.

I subscribe to an e-mail catalog called Shop It To Me. Every other week, I browse great sales and hot clothes, but I've never made a purchase. I simply window shop from my desk. Nothing could be easier than punching in my credit card information and waiting for the product to arrive at my doorstep. But I don't buy because I know the purchase won't really make me happy. It's enough for me to admire. Not buying is my way of fasting, a way of delaying gratification.

Sometimes what we lack is the thrill of anticipation or the delay of gratification. We enjoy things far more when we've really desired them but had to wait for them. The mistake we make is believing that the item holds all the value. The real value is found in our self-control and patience, which allowed us to delay gratification and build anticipation. These qualities can't be purchased. They must be practiced and exercised.

Letting desire build is an abstract way to achieve balance and moderation in your life. Balance and moderation carry negative and boring baggage but really, it's the opposite. When you have one great party of the summer, instead of one every weekend, the event feels original and exciting, and you look forward to doing it again because this is the exception, not the norm. There is anticipation—and sometimes that's better than the actual event!

Moderation just may be the answer to boredom!

Look at something in your life that's losing luster due to routine. Cut it out; see what you do instead. Moderation just may be the answer to boredom—go figure!

Doing Adds Meaning to Life

Nothing has more meaning to us than something we've earned. How would you feel if someone just gave you a gold medal? You didn't train, didn't compete, and didn't earn it; you simply received it. You might think it's cool, but you wouldn't have a deep attachment to it, would you? But trained athletes cherish gold medals they've won, not for the medal itself, but for what the medals represent. The medals are testaments to their dedication to their dreams. They have labored and performed. And their rewards are not just trophies and recognition. They have journeyed through self-discipline, discovery, failure, doubt, experimentation, exposure, change, and, hardest of all, the unknown. That's a long way, and none of that can be taken away from them. That is character, and character has meaning.

Few of us are training to be Olympic athletes, so let's take it down several notches. How about a strawberry patch? You cannot grow a strawberry patch in one season. It takes a couple of years. In fact, the first year it's recommended that you snip all the blossoms to make your plants hardier. Okay, so you delay gratification. And you get some straw so the bugs don't eat your eventual harvest. Then you put up rabbit fencing and bird-proof mesh. Cover the plants during a late frost, and water if there's a drought. Jeez, you could just go to the store and buy some strawberries. And sometimes we do. But what happens when you pick your first full yield? Maybe you make shortcake and invite your friends. Or you make jam and put your name on the label. That's your trophy. Your love, attention, and appreciation

Exercise

Think back to a time when you had to get your head wrapped around something that didn't come easily. Maybe it was deciphering the instruction manual on your bike odometer or installing a railing on a staircase. When have you broken out of your comfort zone to take on a dreadful task and ultimately ended up learning way more than you expected?

Accomplishing one task prepares you for other challenges that will propel your success.

went into every berry. But don't forget, the berries will be back again next year in even greater abundance.

Seeing your plans through to the harvest means you'll have to overcome obstacles and sometimes inner demons. But once you blaze those trails for yourself and come out on the other side, you'll find life gets easier and more plentiful.

When we learn to do things for ourselves—from making a three-tier cake to asking for a promotion to refinishing the basement—we set in motion the awareness that we can continue to expect more. Worlds of possibilities open up. You'll keep asking yourself, "What's next?"

Success can be repeated. Luck and handouts, not so much.

The journey is our real reward, but the end result is what gives the journey meaning. We're not going to labor over a strawberry patch if there aren't going to be any strawberries in the end. The "trophy" is our motivation and the embodiment of our goal. And that's why a trophy means more to the one who earned it than it does to anyone else. Decide what you want your trophy to be and then do all you can to earn it.

Doing Increases Your Magnetism

You can't buy happiness, but you can attract it. How do you attract happiness? First by knowing what makes you happy and then having the courage to pursue those things. As you pursue your happiness, your passion grows. When you're passionate about something, you want to share that something with everyone else. As you start sharing, you'll start attracting like-minded people and forming mutually beneficial relationships. This attracting of like minds is known as human magnetism.

The principles of human magnetism, or laws of attraction, focus on exuding happiness in who you are and what you have, while clearly understanding what you truly desire. People with great magnetism will project excitement for their anticipated joy and diminish feelings of frustration, dislike, and doubt. By embracing positive thoughts and actions, they are met with positive results and outcomes. It becomes a mind-over-matter scenario where decisions are guided by energy moving in the direction of genuine purpose.

You may be wondering why we need to focus on an invisible thing like magnetism. The answer is because it gives you the potential to attract what you need to achieve happiness and well-being. Magnetism can be life changing in regard to your accomplishments and personal relationships. Magnetism creates an energy that brings success and fulfillment.

When I worked at a large consumer products company, I worked with an artsy guy who was frustrated by the rigid systems of corporate culture. He left the package design department of this company to work a data entry job. This looked like a major step down, even career suicide. There is zero creativity in data entry. But he found his new job hypnotically relaxing; it was stress-free. And when he got home, he didn't need to detox from the day with hours of mindless entertainment. He was bursting with creative energy that he could release by painting. He produced a lot of creative work outside the office, including a series of airplane paintings. Then, as fate would have it, he met an executive at Boeing. Because painting is part of who he is, he ended up talking about art and showing the executive some of his work. She loved his paintings and he started selling them for hundreds and thousands of dollars.

It's experiences, not things, that bring true happiness.

This story is magnetism at work. And it started with my former co-worker's courageous decision to shun social convention and leave a career path. Notice he didn't just stop working and start painting full time. He took on a job that paid his bills but left him free time to use his creativity in a way that truly fulfilled him, instead of using his creativity in a system he didn't enjoy. When he made this decision, there was no guarantee that he would ever sell his art. When he left his job, he did it for his own satisfaction, not in pursuit of more money. He actually gave up a lot of career status (and probably some salary), but he found freedom to do what he really loved. To him, being free, happy, and fulfilled was worth more than climbing the corporate ladder. That's a key to the Reduction Rebel lifestyle.

Start Doing Instead of Simply Having

People often find their happiness in the things they have and the things they accumulate during their lifetimes. I would argue that it's experiences, not things, that bring true happiness. Living, creating, laughing, crying, sharing, letting life happen—these experiences are what truly bring meaning to our lives. To illustrate, let me share a story about two successful businessmen who chose different paths with different outcomes.

The Larkin Soap Co. was founded in my hometown of Buffalo, New York, in 1875. Besides its founder, John Larkin, the company had two notable principals: Elbert Hubbard and Darwin Martin. I found an interesting comparison between these two aggressively talented businessmen who emerged from the same company. Martin worked his entire career at the Larkin Co., sometimes working as much as 361 days a year. His outstanding work ethic and contributions to business efficiencies earned him great wealth, which he used to build a mansion designed by Frank Lloyd Wright. But he ultimately died a poor man. When the stock market crashed in 1929, Martin lost millions overnight. Impoverished, he eventually had to walk away from his great home. Literally. He left the doors unlocked and retreated. Today he is best remembered by the home he commissioned Wright to design, not any of his own accomplishments. I find this kind of sad.

> "Character is the result of two things: mental attitude and the way we spend our time."
>
> –ELBERT HUBBARD

Hubbard, on the other hand, left the company in 1875 and, within a few years, embarked on what became an artisan community called The croft. He advocated for the arts-and-crafts community and grew his own little empire. Starting with a printing press, he expanded into handcrafted publications, furniture making, bookbinding, and leather and copper goods. He expanded his operations into a fourteen-building complex. When his community of more than five hundred artisans began drawing public attention from far away places, he had an inn built to house the interested travelers. His enterprise snowballed and took new form as dictated by the continued success of creativity and entrepreneurship. Hubbard died aboard the *RMS Lusitania* in 1915, so we cannot compare how he would have adapted to the stock market crash, though his son continued to run the Roycroft Campus until 1938.

I have great respect for both men, but the end of each ones' story shows how little material possessions matter. Martin lost his house and all he had overnight. Hubbard lost his life in a tragedy, but because he invested in doing and helping others do, his legacy lived on in a meaningful way.

So how can you start doing? How can you tap into the creative energy you have so you are free to create instead of simply consume? Here are some steps to get you started:

Step One: Find What You Love and Give Yourself to It

Remember the story of my former co-worker? He knew being creative and making art was his true passion. Hubbard had a passion for creativity as

Exercise

Think of something you do that causes you to lose all sense of time and discomfort. What relaxes you, but at the same time satisfies? When do you do something that feels good while doing it, and you walk away feeling even better? Do you knit clothing and blankets that you give as gifts? Have you captured your fond memories in a journal or scrapbook? Can you notice improved muscle tone from running the obstacle course at a local park?

Take the time to ponder enjoyable pastimes that have lasting benefits.

well. What are you passionate about? It doesn't have to be something artistic. Maybe it's gardening or baking or organizing social events or volunteering.

If you really don't know, that's okay. Ask yourself, is there something you've always wanted to do, or wished you could do, but you've never been able to do it? If the answer is yes, stop wishing and make it happen. Rearrange your schedule or say no to something else to give yourself time to do this. Otherwise, brainstorm things you would like to try and then carve out intentional time to try them. When you find the right thing, you'll know.

> A fulfilled life is a balance of work and play.

Don't let finances be an issue here. Remember, this is about doing, not consuming, so the thing you want to do should require little financial investment.

When you know what it is you truly love, evaluate your schedule. How much time can you dedicate to this activity? What activities can you give up so you can focus more time on your passion? Do you need to make a lifestyle shift—such as changing jobs—to reclaim more time and energy for living? A fulfilled life is a balance of work and play.

Step Two: Explore a Variety of Interests

We live in the Information Age, and change is coming at us like water shot from a fire hose. To adapt, we need to explore a number of interests. It is A okay to diversity. Go ahead and dip your toe in something different. Don't let the bigwigs keep you from exploring. This isn't about competition, but rather about doing, stretching, and seeing what's out there. Research new fields, talk to different experts. Give new challenges a shot. You'll catch a few breaks and definitely walk away with an experience.

Step Three: Don't Let a Routine Become Your Plan

Routines are comfortable. They set solid rules, expectations, and outcomes. Just like a thirty-year mortgage, you know exactly what you have ahead of you. Many experts advocate for routines, especially with children. Yes, I agree it's healthy and builds confidence in children. I also rely on routines for crunch time, like getting the kids on the bus. I need the regiment to keep us on track.

But let's not confuse routines with planning. A routine is something we do repeatedly. We get up, drink coffee, shower, etc. Planning looks more like: we set out our clothes and make our lunch the night before and double-check that there is milk and cereal for the morning.

The danger of routines is that they are often "set it and forget it." This mentality is fine for some activities, like laundry, grooming, and weekly chores. They need to be done, but they aren't mentally taxing. But establishing routines for creative processes, your career, or even how you use your free time can make you stagnant. When you focus only on the routine, you lose sight of the process—the why and how behind what you are doing.

A plan will help you organize your time and accomplish things while keeping the why and how in mind.

A plan will help you organize your time and accomplish things while keeping the why and how in mind. The great thing about a plan is you can change it. A flexible thinker is able to adapt and create a plan using his skills. When Prohibition hit, some brewers committed suicide, while others made brewer's yeast, ice cream, and nonalcoholic beverages instead. See what I'm saying? Being able to multitask and think on your feet will keep your energy flowing, your problems solved, and your good vibrations radiating.

Exercise

Think about how your consideration of others' needs has attracted positive results in your life. When have you benefited from listening instead of talking? How have your talents accommodated someone else? Giving of ourselves is always reciprocated by the universe, right down to the bonds of friendship and self-accomplishments.

It's a healthy exercise to keep a journal of what you've done. This isn't a way to keep score, but a tool to remind yourself of how far you've come. Jot down the people you've met, lessons learned, skills mastered, emotions felt, and even tips on what to avoid or alternative approaches.

Step Four: Show Genuine Interest in Others

It all comes down to being authentic. When you express your true interests, you reveal your true self. This down-to-earth, relatable version of you is without ego. Ever notice how people with charisma talk with purpose without blabbing about themselves? They actually show more interest in other people. Nothing is gained from talking about yourself, yet so many connections are made from listening.

On the night of the famous Paul Revere ride, another townsman was going door-to-door warning people as well. No one remembers him because he wasn't effective with his warning. Why not? He didn't have rapport with these people. They didn't know to trust his word. He also couldn't call them by name like Revere could. It's not really his fault, but it's interesting to point out why Paul Revere was successful. Revere was a businessman, and not only that, he made things for other people. He was a silversmith who made whatever the customer wanted, including a silver chain for a squirrel. Imagine how that conversation went. He had to surrender all opinions and judgment to accommodate his client. It wasn't about him, only about what he could do for them. That's a powerful shift with amazing results.

New people always bring something to the table. And what you learn from them could be the missing piece that you need to get to the next level, whatever your goal may be. Be intentional about meeting new people who share your passion. Seek out (or start) a club, connect through social media, go to conventions. Be on the lookout. Put out feelers. Strike up conversations. Find common ground and go from there. You cannot grow in a bubble.

Be Willing to Let Go

In chapter three, we talked about getting rid of possessions as a way to organize, make some extra cash, and free up space in our homes. But what about giving things up for the sheer joy of giving? The old saying goes, "It's better to give than to receive." Try it and you'll know. It feels amazing to give someone something that you know they will enjoy—or even as a gesture to say you're thinking about them. This doesn't mean you go out and buy gifts. We all have something in our homes that we keep not because we love it or use it, but because we paid a lot of money for it. This is not a valid reason to hold onto something. Let it go to someone who will love it for what it is, not what it cost. Be glad you had your time with it and move on. See how good it makes you feel. Lose the stuff, feel the love.

Help Others Do for Themselves

We're taught at a young age that actions have consequences. Whether it's punishment, guilt, or bad karma, whenever we take a turn for the worse, it's going to come back to bite us. This is true *unless* there is someone overcompensating for our bad habits. This person makes it possible to avoid the consequences of self-destructive behavior by making excuses or bankrolling mistakes. This person is an enabler. Enabling behavior is commonly seen in parents trying to make up for perceived shortcomings in their parenting or financial obligations to their children. Yes, it's one thing to help someone through a rough patch, but to establish ongoing relief is more harmful than helpful.

> Things and money do not solve problems; education and experience do.

When you buy someone's way out of a problem, you deny that person an opportunity to grow from the situation. I often think back to what would have happened if someone surprised me by furnishing my house. I probably never would have bought my sewing machine or restored my own furniture. Giving denies the need for growth. Being overly generous takes away a person's motivation for independence. If the situation is the result of poor choices, feeling the consequences will teach the person not to repeat those choices in the future. Through preparation, we are able to manage, appreciate, and prosper from what comes into our lives.

Enabling works both ways. Either you're the one wasting your resources on someone who is ill equipped, or you're allowing someone to keep you dependent on them. At the time, you may think it was divine that someone gave you a car, but then the giver expects that you're going to do odd jobs for him around his house. That's not freedom! Have more self-respect than that. You'd be better off riding your bike to work than being under someone else's thumb. Again, it's not fun at first, but neither is weeding someone else's garden. The gift is not worth the misery of its accompanying obligations.

Have you wondered how some lottery winners manage to go broke after winning an incredibly large sum of money? These winners had never learned how to save or manage money. Because they didn't have the proper foundation, they weren't able to handle a large amount of money when they received it. On a similar note, what would happen if you sent me up into space right now? You'd never see me again. You could send me up with the best technology, but because I have no idea how to use it for myself, it would be of no use to me and wouldn't help me return to earth. At the same time, whoever funded my expedition would be out millions. And who would sympathize with them? No one, because they put their goods into the wrong hands. Things and money don't solve problems; education and experience do. The best preparation is practice.

Once you recognize enabling behavior (whether you're the enabler or the one being enabled), create an exit strategy. Notice I didn't say, "Cut that crap out." It's a difficult transition. You have to prepare. You need to set boundaries and deadlines, and find alternative ways to help other than pinch-hitting and financial martyrdom. It's never too late to prepare and educate. Set goals, take small strides, and have some faith—okay, a lot of faith sprinkled with tough love.

Create a Home That Inspires Doing

How does your bedroom make you feel when you first open your eyes in the morning? Do you feel refreshed and ready to face the day, or are you immediately overwhelmed by the clutter and mess around you? What about when you walk into your bathroom or kitchen? Do these areas give you a positive feeling, or do they feel like battlegrounds where you fight chaos and disorder?

Spend time in each room of your home and note how you feel about it. Write down your first impression when you walk in, and then spend a few minutes sitting and observing. Record how you feel after spending time in the room, and then write down how you would like to feel after spending time in the room. Make two lists—one of things you like about the room and the other of things you don't like.

After you complete this exercise, identify what needs to change in the room to create the space you want. Do you need to purge more items from the room? Do you need to move exercise equipment or laundry or crafts to another part of the home? Do you need to dedicate ten minutes each day

Six Steps to Making Guests Feel at Home

1. *Give the grand tour.* You don't have to show off every nook and cranny, but walking guests through the main areas of your home will let your guest know where to find the bathroom and where to throw out their chicken wing bones.

2. *Be up front but polite about your rules.* Guests would much rather you ask that they take their shoes off at the door than have you gasp as they traipse across the carpet. If an armchair is being reserved for an elderly guest, let it be known before you have to awkwardly ask someone to relocate.

3. *Stock necessary supplies.* Weddings aren't the only times to provide your guests with dental floss, breath mints and feminine products. I like to keep a small basket of personal care items in my downstairs bathroom for my guest's use. I also keep a sippy cup and rubber-coated spoon in my kitchen pantry in case I have a toddler in the house. These few provisions take up very little space, yet mean a lot to a guest in need.

4. *Inquire about dietary restrictions ahead of time.* The last thing you want to do is prepare a peanut-crusted meal only to find out a guest has a nut allergy. Equally as devastating is offering a drink to a recovering alcoholic or a steak to a vegetarian. Avoid these host/hostess snafus by asking about any dietary accommodations when you make the invitation so you have plenty of time to plan around them.

5. *Make room for your guests' things.* Yes, you want to make sure your house is free of clutter, but you also want to make sure there is also open space for whatever your guests may bring into your home. Often guests will bring a dish to share. It may need a place in your refrigerator or oven. Make sure you're prepared so it's not a scramble to jam their potato salad between your leftovers and partially filled Tupperware. The same goes for your coat closets and shoe mats. Clear out your goods so your guests don't have their outerwear strewn all over your foyer.

This room has ample seating, a place to rest drinks, and is arranged for socializing.

6. *Create a conversation area.* A vital spark to your room's atmosphere is ample seating arranged circularly. Your living room is a social hub, and proper furniture placement facilitates conversation and comfort. Draw seating close together and around focal points like the piano, fireplace or expansive windows. If rooms have large openings that disrupt the conversation circle, consider adding drapes between openings to enclose the space without cutting it off completely. Be sure to allow enough space between your furniture so people can move about freely. Also provide your guests with a place to set their food or drinks, even if it's a stack of books with a tray on top or a folding TV tray. Guests don't want to get stuck holding their drink all evening. It's all about feeling welcome and comfortable.

to tidying up so the room stays clean and clutter-free? Be bold and let go of the things holding you back in your home. If you hate waking up to the sight of a pile of laundry each morning, set a new rule that laundry isn't allowed in your bedroom. It must stay in the laundry area until it's folded and put away.

It's important that you list the things you like about a room so you can play up those features. Give them prominence in the room. If you need something to improve the function or beauty of the room, make a list of what you need and be on the lookout for things you can upcycle to meet those needs. Surf the web for inexpensive inspiration.

Whatever you do, don't make the mistake of thinking brand-new furniture or decorations will change the way you feel about or care for a room when the real problem is you're drowning in clutter. It doesn't matter how expensive your coffee table is if you can never see the top of it. Address the clutter problem first by finding proper homes for things and putting stuff away after you use it. Then consider upcycling the table by giving it a new coat of paint or decorative finish. You'll enjoy it so much more because you'll appreciate all the work you put into keeping it clear and making it beautiful. Besides, what happens when you buy an eight thousand dollar dining room set and you're still making payments on it? You want people to just look at it, like it is a showroom, right? You don't want anyone to use it for fear that it will be damaged? That mentality doesn't say home; it says catalog or store, like you took the display and moved it to your house. You and your guests will be on pins and needles because you don't want to disturb the perfection or damage something.

If your home is truly welcoming to you, it will be welcoming to others as well. When you enjoy your home, you'll automatically want to welcome other people into it. When you set up (and work) a plan to keep your home organized and clean, you'll always feel energized, and you'll never have to dread inviting people over. You'll feel free to host coffee or dinner parties at home instead of going out to a restaurant.

> It's important that you list the things you like about a room so you can play up those features.

The "Me" in Game

There was an episode of *The Wonder Years* where the main character, Kevin, became obsessed with the star of the school's basketball team. His grades slipped while he remained in loyal attendance at all the games. In the end, the team lost in the finals. While the star was sulking, Kevin tried to cheer him up by saying, "We wouldn't have gotten this far if it hadn't been for you."

The basketball player looked at him and said, "We?"

Ouch, that's harsh, but it's true. Watching a game is not playing it. The audience has no affect on the outcome. They are just clapping bystanders. The outcome of a sporting event has virtually no affect on the world. It's purely live entertainment. But what if I asked how you felt about the outcome of your life? That's a different story. That does have meaning and can affect the world. That's why we cannot sit back and be content that we know people who are successful. Tagging along, riding coattails, and just getting by are not going to cut it. We must experience our own success in order to be happy.

> We must experience our own success in order to be happy.

If you're not feeling sustained happiness, ask yourself why you may be clinging to the sidelines. Is it fear, comfort, distractions, or indecision? No one says you have to get it right the first time. But what you will get the first time is experience that will guide your next decision.

Please don't expect conditions to be perfect, either. The game of life doesn't come with a grounds keeper who will perfectly mow the field and mark the lines. You just have to get out there, face your opponents, and use all you've got to win. That's how heroes are made.

7: Love the Process

A tour of Boston took me past a brick warehouse that, according to the tour guide, was used by a woman to store the furniture she had collected on her world travels. Crates containing the treasures she had found and shipped home were stacked floor to ceiling. She continued to travel and collect for many years. When she finally returned to rediscover her exotic, global merchandise, she found that the boxes contained nothing but sawdust. Termites had destroyed her lifelong accumulations. What do you conclude from this story?

It reminds me that things are just things, and they can be destroyed, stolen, or taken away at any time. I hope the woman took the time to savor her travel in the foreign lands and that she learned about other cultures, met new people, and experienced the adventure of the conquest. If she did, she did not lose the most valuable souvenirs of her travels. Her experiences could never be taken away, and they could be relived every day in her memory. The story reminds me that our experiences will always bring a richness to our lives that can never be erased, and it's far more important to invest in relationships and experiences than material things.

As you worked through the concepts and projects in this book, you may have felt like it was you against rubbish. But when you sit back and look at the beauty that surrounds you, you'll remember the kind woman to whom you sold your stained-glass window or the beaming bride-to-be who bought your wedding gown. Your coffee table will have a story to tell, and your garage will host a gathering of new friends that you met at your neighborhood garage sale. This is what you get from simplifying your life, cleaning out your house, and paying off debt. It feels a lot like satisfaction, and that is awesome.

The Pleasures of Planning

Planning a major event is a lot of work and requires a ton of dedication. Whether you're organizing a family reunion, wedding, fund-raiser, or corporate picnic, you know there are scattered pieces that need to come together in perfect harmony. We go to great lengths to accomplish our goals of making everything run smoothly and ensuring everyone has a great time. Therefore, seeing it come to fruition is something to be cherished. But don't forget to cherish all the effort you put into it because, in the process, you find all of the small wins that keep you going every day.

The reduction lifestyle takes some planning, too. First and foremost, we have to think about how we want to live. What do we want in our homes and on our schedules? How do we want to spend our time, and with whom do we want to spend it? The planning stage is our time to fantasize about how full and productive our lives can be. We can sort out what is meaningful, necessary, and inspiring. Exploring life's greater possibilities is so exhilarating because they are endless.

Part of the planning phase involves detachment. You'll be separating yourself from the pack. Please don't look at it as loneliness or isolation. This is a transition from where you don't want to be to where you are free to live exactly as you want. You're simply getting rid of the junk in your life.

Facilitating a Positive Outcome

1. *Be open to possibilities.* I always like to ask around to get ideas. When I know someone else has done something, that something becomes much more real to me, and I believe I can do it, too. Be open to new and better solutions. Run them through your values filter and decide what is right for you.

2. *Clear your thoughts.* Before you can focus on a plan, you need to let all the little gnats in your life fade away. Try to connect to nature through eco therapy (spending time outdoors). It's amazing how putting ourselves in nature helps us sort out our thoughts, relax, and detoxify. We gain clarity on what's bothering us and what really brings happiness. Our thoughts are free to evolve into plans as we work through our emotions without forced stimulus.

3. *Create a vision board.* The things you look at and regularly behold have unbelievable power over your mood and the choices you make. Surrounding yourself with positive images of your ideal life, home, occupation and habits will help you gravitate to those things in real life. Add positive messages along with pictures to remind you of the goals you are working toward and the strong assets within you that will help you reach those goals.

4. *Regularly visualize the positive outcome in your head.* Close your eyes and imagine yourself reaching your goal. Envision entertaining guests in your clean, organized home. Imagine writing a check to pay off your debt. See your projects through to completion in your mind. The more you play out the scenarios in your head, the more your subconscious is trained to believe it's actually happening. And then it does happen.

Categories for a Vision Board

1. *Natural Attractions:* These are things you feel represent a natural part of your personality. What do you look at and say, "That is so me"?
2. *Everyday Moments:* Think of small, daily experiences you would like to have, like sharing a meal with your family or relaxing in a comfy chair in the sun. Clip images that align with the situations that you want to emulate.
3. *Goals:* We all strive to be better, but what exactly will your goals look like? Explore the visual outcomes of all your goals—spiritual, financial, physical, personal development, and domestic.

There should be no farewell tears over that! Say sayonara to your rut, and say hello to reemerging as a whole new you. Take immense pleasure in thinking about your leap of emotional status. Think about how you want to look on the other side. Where are you going to spend your time, talents, and money?

Like any great event, a theme ties this all together. As a Reduction Rebel, your theme is freedom. You know the plan you are chasing—one that cuts out stress, hassles, and obstacles. And the best thing about planning is that you can start from anywhere. You can be young, old, busy, bored—it doesn't matter; all that matters is that you're getting the wheels in motion. Better things are on the way. You'll literally feel the exhilaration of anticipation and the thrill of positive change. Just be sure to commit to the change. Accept the idea of the next step, the bigger wave. Because when the waste, clutter, stress, and debt come off, you are free to skyrocket into your ideal life.

The Power of Discovery

The gateway to discovery is saying yes to challenges. By deviating off the path of the expected and already exposed, you position yourself to gain knowledge and uncover new personal discoveries. These discoveries come in the form of new interests, talents, skills, and creative ideas. Discovery happens every time you try something new. It's improvising, exploring, connecting, and seeking.

Three Challenges That Lead to Discovery

1. *Try something new.* Let go of inhibitions and false limitations and open yourself to new experiences. Seek the help of someone who has already been there, done that, and have them walk you through the process. You will discover an awareness and ability within yourself that broadens your horizons and takes away stress and apprehension.

2. *Change the application.* You start to think differently when you look at things differently. By repurposing methods and products, you discover new resources and applications that simplify and streamline life.

3. *Dig deeper.* It's so easy to take things at face value. A task or item looks unappealing, difficult, or inconvenient, therefore it is unappealing, difficult, or inconvenient. By taking the time to investigate for potential and silver linings, you can really surprise yourself in a great way.

Give yourself permission to be creative and look for new ways to do things. Be curious. You may find a new, better way to do something, or you may find a way not to do something. A failed experiment can be just as valuable as a successful one if you learn from it.

What does discovery look like, and how do you open yourself up to it? Discovery looks a lot like hands-on curiosity. Engage with the world around you. Get your hands dirty exploring topics new to you. If you read or hear about something that piques your interest, try it yourself; don't just be a spectator. You can buy organic produce from the store, or you can discover the full benefit of local organic food by growing your own organic garden. A garden requires more work, but it saves you money and reduces your consumption, which helps the environment by reducing packaging and shipping. When something becomes obsolete in your home, don't give up on it. Brainstorm ways to upcycle it and make it functional, either for yourself or someone else.

There is an unbelievable pride of ownership when we are at the origin of something great. Connecting the dots and bringing all the pieces together turn on your internal light bulb, and that creative light will shine from within you on everything you have and everyone you meet. The more you do, the more motivated you are to continue doing. You will want to build on your involvement by setting higher goals and applying your learning to other endeavors. The emotions manifested inside you catch fire and spread to all areas of your life. You will be the fuel to take what you have in front of you and make it better. Discover what you are capable of—it's probably more than you ever dreamed.

We are Neither the Beginning nor the End

I once saw a show about beautiful estates in America. One owner who was interviewed for the show called himself the "steward of the home," as opposed to the owner. He explained that the home was here long before him and will remain long after him. Hmmm. Isn't that true of everything? What comes into our lives is not really ours; it's just ours to take care of for a certain amount of time. Even our children who were born out of our own bodies will grow up and live on without us.

Does this perspective change your attachment to the things in your life? Attachment is where problems occur. Our needs control us. When you can't live without something, you've lost control over that thing, and it now controls you. Is it worth sacrificing your freedom to an object? Isn't an object meant to serve you instead of you serving it?

Recognize that things come in and out of our lives every day. They rarely start with us and rarely end with us. You have a temporary amount of time with them. So what do we do with these things? Enjoy them, preserve them, appreciate them, or improve them. After you've done one or all of these things, pass them on to someone else who will do the same. Don't let the things you hold onto hold you back.

We are simply guardians of history, preserving and advancing what has come into our lives—knowledge and possessions alike. We make a difference with every seedling we nurture, table we restore, helpful tip we share, and heirloom we carefully pass on to the next generation.

The Value of Appreciation

If you've ever watched *Antiques Roadshow* or *American Pickers*, you know the appraisers almost always say something like, "Thank you for letting me see this." They get joy just from seeing the item. They don't have to own it; it's enough that they could examine it.

Appreciation is a huge part of the Reduction Rebel lifestyle. Appreciation awakens you to the blessings of the moment. It helps you be aware of what you're experiencing, who you're meeting, and how you're participating.

When your attitude is focused on appreciation, you're thinking about the positive. This helps you take one small success and grow from there. You recognize opportunities, quality, and significance, which make the results all the more valuable. What you appreciate, you care for effortlessly and selflessly. Appreciation improves your mood and puts you into receiving mode. And just imagine what will flow into your life as you acquire numerous skills and interests, and more free space in your house.

Imagine what will flow into your life as you acquire numerous skills and interests, and more free space in your house.

During the time my husband and I were slowly and systematically furnishing our home, we reserved a large corner of our living room for a baby grand piano we hoped to acquire in the future. We had the space and the need (my husband is a very talented pianist). We just needed the instrument. We knew we'd get one; we just didn't know when or how, until we arrived home one night and listened to a phone message from my sister. She told us that her church was giving away a piano to whomever was willing to pay to move it. Jackpot. We jumped at the chance. Now don't think this piano was shiny, elegant, or in tune. It had an alligator finish and was missing a key. But that was not what we saw. We saw a 1922 Knabe baby grand piano that would fit perfectly in our home; an instrument that would become the focal point of our home; a tool for my husband to create his music.

Next came the true test of appreciation: research. I've found that the more you appreciate something, the more you want to know about it. It's true of people you respect, art you admire, and things that really tickle your fancy. So we researched our piano and found that the "Star Spangled

Banner" was composed on a Knabe piano. I also discovered that our piano had been used in the grammar school I attended. It was the piano I listened to through nine years of music class. (Now there's a bit of a coincidental connection that validates that it was meant to be.) This story shows how the culmination of planning, discovery, appreciation, and ultimately acceptance streamlines abundance in life. If we hadn't planned to have a piano and then intentionally left space for it (even though we knew we couldn't afford one any time soon), we wouldn't have been able to accept the piano when it was being given away. If we hadn't shared our plans with others, my sister wouldn't have known to contact me about the piano. If we didn't believe in the power of restoration, we would have written off the damaged, out-of-tune piano as unusable. And if I hadn't researched the piano's history, I would have missed out on connecting it to my past.

Create space in your own life for the things you want, whether they are possessions or experiences. Share these desires with others. Gratefully receive what comes your way and watch what happens!

The Rewards of Being a Reduction Rebel

Before I start anything, I like to take the time to think about where I am and where I'm going. I think about the people I've yet to meet and the new experiences I've yet to discover. This gets me really excited, almost as excited as seeing my progress. Yes, progress: that moment when we stop the drip in our shower, finally pay off a loan, or bake a soufflé that doesn't sink in the middle. It's all part of the transition from being tied down to living fancy-free.

Becoming a Reduction Rebel is a right of passage celebrated through many milestones of success. These milestones occur financially, intellectually, and socially. Get thrilled about each and every one of them. This is no small feat. You need to be rip-roaring psyched!

Debt-Free

Until the mid-nineteenth century, people with outstanding debt could be sent to debtor prisons until their family could pay off their debt. This concept seems unbelievable to us today, seeing how so many people carry tons of debt. But is this prison concept so far-fetched? As long as you have debt, you're working to pay someone else, plus interest. You may not be living in a single cell with a bunch of diseased strangers, but you are still not free.

Often, we feel something makes sense because a majority of people are doing it. Not true. It doesn't make sense to live your life owing your paycheck to someone else. Someday, the majority will say they want more out of life and that they don't want debt that lasts half their lives. You are on the ground floor of this emerging majority.

I was interviewed for an article in the August 2010 issue of *Money* magazine where I talked about how my husband and I paid off our house when we were thirty-four. My neighbor saw the article, and he told me he did the same thing. A work associate of mine who lives halfway across the country called to say he read the article and was in the same boat as us. It was very cool to know change was emerging.

How does this change happen? By getting jacked when you pay off debt, when you cut out costly, unrewarding expenditures, and when you make some extra cash on stuff that's weighing you down. It's a fabulous, contagious feeling. Believe me, you'll want to do it again and again, just like anything that feels 100 percent good.

Higher Learning

School graduations are a pretty ubiquitous rite of passage in our society. We have formal graduation starting in nursery school and continuing through graduate school. But what happens after graduation is what's most important. We forge ahead and evolve and adapt by seeking the knowledge we need to thrive. Our continuing pursuit of higher levels of thinking is then celebrated not in a ceremony, but in everyday life through self-sufficiency and self-expression. As we ingest more information, we are able to achieve more. Knowledge achieves satisfaction, and satisfaction achieves peace of mind. Cheers to that!

Loving what you do and who surrounds you factor into celebrating a long, healthy life. And the best way to keep the love flowing is to keep finding ways to express yourself creatively and cast about for new experiences.

There was a time in my life when I was working so many hours that I felt like every day was the same. I remember telling myself, "I can get old really fast with this routine." I was in my early twenties at the time, but I knew how fast high school and college blew by, pounding the books, living on campus, looking at the same scene day in and day out. Yeah, even though I was learning, discovery wasn't in the mix. Life got a lot more satisfying when I slowed down and developed my talents with the intention of happiness. These were the real milestones worth jumping up and down about.

Stretch your mind to a point of health and happiness because knowledge is power. And ignorance isn't bliss; it's unfulfilling.

Deeper Social Connections

Let's ponder the social benefits you'll experience as a Reduction Rebel. Being a jack-of-all-trades helps you connect with people at all levels. Think about it. The more diverse your knowledge, the more common ground you will have with the people you meet. Forget awkward introductions or gaps in conversation; you're now far more interesting than your former self. You can talk about the things you're learning, discoveries you're making, and experiences you're having. Stay humble and make the experience, not yourself, the center of the conversation (no one wants to hear about you; they want to hear about the process so they can try it, too). There is a reason you've brought yourself into the company of so many new people—to make positive connections. Talk about things that are interesting to you, and others will feel that interest.

To see the other social benefit, look around your house. What do you see? A place you're über proud of. Maybe you're already thinking, *book club at my house!* Now that you've trimmed down the clutter, put everything neatly in place and created spaces for doing, you are raring to go. Send out the e-vites. Pull out your apron. Bring home the good times!

This is the new you, and you've made it all happen.

Index

Dedication
To Patrick, Pad and Bears—we stick together.

About the Author
Cristin Frank earned a Bachelor's Degree in design from the Rochester Institute of Technology before spending thirteen years in branding and marketing for consumer products, such as Budweiser, Nestlé, Kraft, and SC Johnson. Since 2002, Cristin has been upcycling curbside trash into interior design treasures. This crafty mom has a creative reuse for anything from old T-shirts to a dismantled dresser. In 2009, she founded Eve of Reduction, a lifestyle movement encompassing upcycling, consumption control, and simple living. Her message is clear. "Use your talents and creativity, not consumption, to find personal satisfaction."

She has been published in *FamilyFun Magazine*. Cristin's reduction lifestyle platform continues to attract media attention. Her story and projects have been featured in *Money* magazine, NPR Marketplace Money, CNNMoney.com, and HGTV.com.

For more information on the Reduction Rebel lifestyle and upcycling inspiration, visit EveofReduction.com. For exclusive features, sign up on the website for the Reduction Rebel free e-newsletter.

To book Cristin Frank for a speaking engagement, visit http://www.eveofreduction.com/contact.

Acknowledgments
I want to thank the team at Betterway Home Books for giving me the opportunity to write this book. A special thank you to my editor, Jackie, who provided spot-on guidance that made this book stronger. I would also like to extend my gratitude to the designer, Clare, who coached me through the photography like a rock star. You both made this process an unbelievably cherished experience.

Personally speaking, I thank my husband, Patrick, who has partnered with me on everything I value in this world.

ISBN: 978-1-4403-2525-0

Other fine Betterway Home Books are available from your local bookstore or online or direct from the publisher. Visit our website, www.betterwaybooks.com.

17   16   15   14   13   5   4   3   2

Distributed in Canada by Fraser Direct
100 Armstrong Avenue, Georgetown, Ontario, Canada L7G 5S4, Tel: (905) 877-4411

Distributed in the U.K. and Europe by F&W Media International, LTD
Brunel House, Forde Close, Newton Abbot, TQ12 4PU, UK, Tel: (+44) 1626 323200,
Fax: (+44) 1626 323319, E-mail: enquires@fwmedia.com

Distributed in Australia by Capricorn Link
P.O. Box 704, S. Windsor NSW, 2756 Australia, Tel: (02) 4560-1600,
Fax: (02) 4577-5288, E-mail: books@capricornlink.com.au

Photography by Cristin Frank
Edited by Jacqueline Musser
Designed by Clare Finney
Production coordinated by Debbie Thomas